Psychodynamic Art Practice with People on the Autistic Spectrum

Psychodynamic Art Therapy Practice with People on the Autistic Spectrum offers a valuable counterbalance to the phenomenological, cognitive and behavioural theories that currently prevail in the wider field of practice and research. The result of a decade of work by a group of highly experienced art therapists, this book presents eight frank and compelling accounts of art therapy with either adults or children with autism, supported by a discussion of the relevant theory.

The book begins with an overview of the theoretical context and the subsequent chapters give varied accounts of practitioners' experiences structured in a loose developmental arc, reflecting issues that may arise in different settings and at various stages of therapy. Each is followed by an afterword that describes the author's reflections in light of their experience. The conclusion ties together some of the common threads from their encounters and considers how these themes might be relevant to current and continuing art therapy practice in the field of autism. *Psychodynamic Art Therapy Practice with People on the Autistic Spectrum* is a thoughtful consideration of where art therapy meets autism and the particular challenges that arise in the encounter between the autistic client and the therapist.

Presenting honest reflections arising from lived encounters and highlighting general principles and experiences, this book aims to orient other practitioners who work with people on the autistic spectrum, in particular art therapists and art therapy trainees.

Matt Dolphin has over 20 years' experience in social care and special education. He works with people with learning difficulties as an art therapist and visual arts lecturer and is a member of the British Association of Art Therapists.

Angela Byers is an art therapist and group psychotherapist. At present she works in the NHS as an art therapy clinician, supervisor and manager. She was also a visiting tutor at Goldsmith's College, University of London.

Alison Goldsmith worked as an art therapist in adult mental health services for some years and has taught on the MA art therapy course at the University of Hertfordshire. She has an MA in Jung and Post-Jungian Studies and is a psychoanalytic psychotherapist with experience in the NHS and private practice.

Ruth E. Jones has worked with adults, children, families and organisations as an art therapist, psychotherapist, supervisor and consultant in the NHS, special education, charitable and private sectors since qualifying in the early 1990s.

Psychodynamic Art Therapy Practice with People on the Autistic Spectrum

Edited by Matt Dolphin,
Angela Byers, Alison Goldsmith and
Ruth E. Jones

Routledge
Taylor & Francis Group
LONDON AND NEW YORK

First published 2014
by Routledge
27 Church Road, Hove, East Sussex BN3 2FA

Simultaneously published in the USA and Canada
by Routledge
711 Third Avenue, New York, NY 10017

Routledge is an imprint of the Taylor & Francis Group, an informa business

© 2014 Matt Dolphin, Angela Byers, Alison Goldsmith and Ruth E. Jones.

The right of the editors to be identified as the author of the editorial material, and of the authors for their individual chapters, has been asserted in accordance with sections 77 and 78 of the Copyright, Designs and Patents Act 1988.

All rights reserved. No part of this book may be reprinted or reproduced or utilised in any form or by any electronic, mechanical, or other means, now known or hereafter invented, including photocopying and recording, or in any information storage or retrieval system, without permission in writing from the publishers.

Trademark notice: Product or corporate names may be trademarks or registered trademarks, and are used only for identification and explanation without intent to infringe.

British Library Cataloguing in Publication Data
A catalogue record for this book is available from the British Library

Library of Congress Cataloging in Publication Data
Psychodynamic art therapy practice with people on the autistic spectrum / edited by Matt Dolphin, Angela Byers, Alison Goldsmith, and Ruth E. Jones.
pages cm
ISBN 978-0-415-52393-6 (hardback) – ISBN 978-0-415-52394-3 (pbk.) -- ISBN 978-0-203-76268-4 (ebook) 1. Autism spectrum disorders in children--Treatment. 2. Autism spectrum disorders--Treatment. 3. Art therapy. 4. Psychodynamic psychotherapy. I. Dolphin, Matt. II. Byers, Angela. III. Goldsmith, Alison. IV. Jones, Ruth E. (Psychotherapist)
RC553.A88P77 2013
616.89'1656--dc23
2013008802

ISBN: 978-0-415-52393-6 (hbk)
ISBN: 978-0-415-52394-3 (pbk)
ISBN: 978-0-203-76268-4 (ebk)

Typeset in Times
by Saxon Graphics Ltd, Derby

Printed and bound in Great Britain by
TJ International Ltd, Padstow, Cornwall

This book is dedicated to Rita Simon (1921–2008), and to all the autistic individuals, their parents and families and involved professionals who have made our learning possible.

Contents

	List of contributors	*ix*
	Preface	*xi*
	Acknowledgements	*xiii*
1	**Introduction**	1
2	**Frozen in headlights: working with loss in art therapy with a man with Asperger's Syndrome** MATT DOLPHIN	19
3	**Emptiness and silence: art therapy with a child with autism** SUE GINSBERG	35
4	**A group of five autistic young adults** PENELOPE WILSON	51
5	**Rhythm and flow: re-thinking art therapy with an autistic young man** ANGELA BYERS	65
6	**Images and imagination: a Jungian approach to art therapy with an autistic woman** ALISON GOLDSMITH	75
7	**A collaborative art therapy approach** ELIZABETH ASHBY	89

8	**It is joy to be hidden but disaster not to be found: art therapy with a girl diagnosed with autism** RUTH E. JONES	105
9	**Adolescence and autonomy: art therapy with a young adult with autistic spectrum disorder** LESLEY ANNE MOORE	119
10	**Contemporary views and ways forward for future practice**	133
	Index	*151*

Contributors

Elizabeth Ashby works in the NHS in the Midlands with people who have learning disabilities and older people. She is currently studying for a Ph.D., having also gained an M.Res., and is concerned about the need for a strong evidence base for art therapy.

Angela Byers Dip. AD art and design; PG Diploma in Art Therapy; PG Diploma in Group Psychotherapy; M.Sc. in Social Research Methods; she has worked in health and social services and published about art therapy with older people.

Matt Dolphin has over 20 years' experience in social care and special education. He gained his art therapy qualification from the University of Hertfordshire in 2000, and currently works with people with learning difficulties as an art therapist and visual arts lecturer.

Sue Ginsberg is a registered art therapist currently working in special education in Hertfordshire. She is also an artist. Before training as an art therapist she was an early years teacher specialising in learning difficulties and autism.

Alison Goldsmith has over 20 years' art therapy experience in adult mental health services in the public sector. She has taught on the MA art therapy courses at the University of Hertfordshire and Roehampton University and has supervised art therapy practitioners. She has an MA in Jung and Post-Jungian Studies and is a psychoanalytic psychotherapist with experience in the NHS and private practice.

Ruth E. Jones is a psychoanalytic psychotherapist at the Riverside Practice in Kent. She has over 18 years' experience working with adults, children, families and organisations as an art therapist, psychotherapist, supervisor and consultant in the NHS, special education, charitable and private sectors.

Lesley Anne Moore studied Fine Art at Winchester School of Art, and went on to complete a Masters in Fine Art in Manchester. Once qualified as an art therapist in 2002, from the University of Hertfordshire, she relocated to Dorset and worked in inpatient and community services. She has worked in adult mental health for 16 years, mainly within the National Health Service.

Penelope Wilson qualified as an art therapist at the University of Hertfordshire in 1994. Her main area of professional experience has been with children and adolescents in schools. From 1994 to 2004 she worked for Croydon Educational Psychology Service and at a Special School. Subsequently she worked for Kids Company and privately from home. For the past three years she has co-run the Foundation Course in Art Psychotherapy at Goldsmith's College.

Preface

This book is the result of a decade of work by art therapists who have met as a group to share their thinking about the experience and meaning of art therapy with clients on the autistic spectrum.

In the mid 1990s there was an increase in both the diagnosis of and provision of specialist educational services for children with autism. With this acknowledgement of autism and autistic spectrum disorders as a distinct condition, resources were specifically earmarked for this discrete population. As art therapists already employed to work with clients with learning disabilities and in special education, we found ourselves increasingly being asked to offer art therapy to those affected by autism.

The work presented here is mainly from the psychodynamic/psychoanalytic tradition of art therapy practice; within this, however, we find diverse voices, styles and theoretical content. The chapters, many of which were first delivered as talks at two Somerset House conferences entitled 'Images and the Emergence of Meaning' organised by our group in 2000 and 2002, have been written in a spirit of frank and rigorous exploration rather than in the context of evidence-based practice or empirical research. We would argue that case studies can be both a useful tool for teaching and learning and a valuable addition to qualitatively-based research.

Given our retrospective position, the introduction will contextualise our work in the light of the research and literature available at the time. Each chapter is followed by an afterword in which the writer considers their earlier work with the benefit of hindsight.

We then survey theoretical changes over the past decade within art therapy and consider new approaches that have influenced practice and thinking in the field.

Our aim is to write candidly and moments of struggle and crisis are acknowledged; sometimes these moments point the way forward to evolving forms of practice. Many art therapists today are adapting to new ways of working with an increasing bias towards interactive models and an emphasis on observable phenomena rather than the more receptive stance of the psychodynamic approach to unconscious processes.

In this book we share our perspective as art therapists trying to make the necessary adjustments to prevailing art therapy practice in the context of increasing knowledge and understanding of the nature of autism, yet without losing our own sense of identity and purpose.

Acknowledgements

We would like to thank Robin Tipple and Lesley Fox for their generous support of the group over many years and for their contribution towards shaping the ideas in this book.

Liz Ashby's thanks go to the Music, Drama and Speech and Language Therapy colleagues with whom she developed the work she has described and to Colin's carer for giving permission to use the images and text.

The excerpt in Sue Ginsberg's chapter from the poem 'The Beast in the Space' by W.S. Graham is printed with kind permission of Michael Snow, literary executor of W.S. Graham's estate.

Ruth E. Jones' developmental schema was originally published in the European Journal of Psychotherapy, Counselling and Health, 1998 and reprinted in *Our Desire of Unrest: Thinking About Therapy* by Michael Jacobs (published in 2009). It is reprinted here with kind permission of the publishers, Taylor and Francis Ltd, www.tandfonline.com and Karnac Books respectively.

Cover acknowledgement: Image from a drawing by 'Elizabeth' (chapter 8), reproduced with the kind permission of her parents.

Chapter 1

Introduction

This book begins with an overview of the theoretical context at the end of the twentieth century and looks at how art therapists have approached their work with people on the autistic spectrum. The main section gives varied accounts of practitioners' experiences 'on the ground' and is structured in a loose developmental arc, reflecting issues that may arise in different settings and at different stages of therapy. The chapters in this section mostly concern work that was done before our two Somerset House 'Images and the Emergence of Meaning' conferences in 2000 and 2002, and each account is followed by an afterword written in 2012, which introduces the author's further reflections. The third and concluding section surveys developments in theory and practice since the turn of the millennium. It brings together some of the common threads arising from our case studies and considers how these might be relevant to current art therapy practice in the field of autism, including an acknowledgement of 'neurodiversity'.

In this introductory chapter we present a brief description of the condition of autism, its clinical presentation and a consideration of the particular ways in which art therapists use imagination and a shared symbolic language, for instance in addressing the characteristic triad of impairments (Wing, 1981). We include a review of the psychoanalytic theories and concepts referred to by authors in the book, and a description of theories of symbol formation.

A summary of the literature about art therapy with people on the autistic spectrum that was published before 2000 will precede a brief description of the case studies and their most significant themes.

Autism – the background

While it is beyond the scope of this book to provide an in-depth clinical description of autism, it is helpful to provide an overview. An understanding of the characteristics that may be displayed by people on the autistic spectrum can help to orient the practitioner, particularly if the focus of the work is on communication, the use of the imagination, aesthetics or interpersonal relationships.

Defining a syndrome

The psychiatrist Leo Kanner is usually credited with the first clinical account of autism as we understand it today. He described eight boys and three girls, paying particular attention to their interpersonal relationships, their language development and their interaction with the environment (Kanner, 1943: 217–50). His case reports highlight the children's aloofness and indifference to others, traits that were present from the beginning of life. Kanner recognised that the children he described as autistic were not lacking in emotion but had a disturbance of affective contact. He makes a clear distinction between the affective disturbance of autism and that of schizophrenia, saying of autism that it is 'a fundamental disorder in the children's *inability to relate themselves* in the ordinary way to people and situations from the beginning of life'. He distinguishes this from schizophrenic psychopathology by saying of autism that 'it is not a "withdrawal" from a formerly existing participation. There is from the start an *"extreme autistic aloneness"'* (Kanner, 1943: 242).

Also characteristic were a lack of spontaneity in play, an absence or unusual use of language and a desire for the 'maintenance of sameness' (Kanner, 1943: 245). Kanner applied the word 'autism' to the emerging syndrome, a term that had been coined (from the Greek 'autos', meaning 'self') by Swiss psychiatrist Eugen Bleuler in relation to schizophrenic self-absorption and withdrawal (Bleuler, 1908).

While Kanner conducted his research in the USA, his contemporary Hans Asperger was investigating a different group of children in his Viennese clinic. These youngsters – to whom Asperger (1944) applied the term 'autistic psychopathy' – were similarly socially isolated and averse to change. However, they were distinguished from Kanner's subjects by their cognitive and linguistic development, which was at or beyond what could normally be expected. But their use of language was odd, with (for example) an over-formal or disembodied quality. Asperger noted that these idiosyncrasies could find expression in the form of originality in thought and perception.

Like Kanner, the children Asperger wrote about were not lacking in affect; they could, for example, display extreme grief and homesickness. However, there seemed to be a disjunction between affect and intellect, which disrupted their relationships with others and their understanding of the emotional norms that regulate social conduct.

Kanner's descriptions, written in English, were initially more influential in forming the diagnostic criteria for autism, as his work was enlarged and elaborated upon into the 1970s. In 1978 Michael Rutter created a new definition of 'childhood autism' (Rutter, 1978), which drew attention to the fact that many autistic children were also affected by global developmental delay impacting upon all areas of cognitive functioning. The diagnostic manual *Diagnostic and Statistical Manual of Mental Disorders* (DSM-III) (American Psychiatric Association, 1980) placed autism in a new category of 'pervasive developmental disorders'.

Autism as a spectrum

In 1980 Asperger's papers were published in English and began to influence practitioners in the autism field. Among them were Lorna Wing and Judy Gould, who had been studying children attending special schools or classes in South London. They observed a pattern of presenting difficulties that allowed them to formulate a continuum of autistic features. They saw traits displaying a recognisable commonality but varying in expression and severity according to the personality, skills and cognitive ability of each individual. This has become known as the autistic (or autism) spectrum.

Wing and Gould gave shape to these commonalities by delineating a three-way pattern or *triad* of impairments, which has been influential in informing both the diagnostic criteria for autism (American Psychiatric Association, 1994; World Health Organization, 1992) and subsequent clinical interventions:

- absence or impairment of genuine two-way social interaction;
- problems with comprehension and the use of language, particularly in the realm of 'iconic' communication (non-verbal language and pragmatics, the idiomatic application of speech);
- an unusual quality of imaginative activity, and a narrow range of repetitive interests or pursuits, often taking the place of flexible, co-operative play.

The first of these criteria is subdivided into a 'mini-triad', based upon the individual's approach to interaction: aloof – passive – active but odd (Wing and Attwood, 1987).

Importantly – and somewhat controversially – the concept of a spectrum allows for the inclusion of 'high-functioning' autism and Asperger's Syndrome, in which difficulties associated with Wing's triad are present but there is no discernible cognitive delay (indeed, some abilities may be enhanced and highly developed). A debate continues over whether there is a need for these two separate terms. Tony Attwood, for example, concludes that there is no clear reason to make a distinction and that the education and support available to both groups would be similar (Attwood, 2003). Psychiatrist Fred Volkmar notes that diagnosis is more problematic when assessment criteria are applied to people with very high or very low cognitive abilities (Volkmar, 1998). There is a related question of the overlap – or not – between autism and cognitive learning disabilities (see, for example, Chapter 7 of this book).

Central Coherence Theory

Alongside the derivation of the term 'autism', accounts of work with autistic people in this book and elsewhere suggest an absence or fragility of self as a central ordering principle. In her Central Coherence Theory, psychologist Uta Frith (1989) contends that this is the chief deficit in autism, with all other manifestations of the condition stemming from it. Perception and cognition are atomistic rather than global, so that the concepts or 'gestalts' that would normally give meaning to experience are lost in a welter of detail. Frith's conception may be supported by the way that some autistic people experience unbearably heightened sensory responses. This impartial or undifferentiated kind of seeing can also lead to exceptional abilities and originality in some autists. Temple Grandin's life and pioneering work as a designer of systems for the humane handling and slaughter of livestock was the subject of a recent biopic (director Mick Jackson, 2010). Grandin, a prodigiously gifted visual thinker who also experiences sensory hypersensitivity, has said that most people seem to test existing theories against reality whereas she uses (concrete) reality to move slowly towards the formation of concepts (Sacks, 1995: 270).

Relationships and theory of mind

Simon Baron-Cohen, Alan Leslie and Uta Frith (1985) have suggested that people with autism do not employ a theory of mind, and so have difficulty attributing desires, beliefs and intentions to others when they interact with them. This capacity is termed a 'theory' because the mind of the other is not empirically testable through observation; rather it is a construct based on analogy with one's own mind and deductions about the motives underlying others' behaviour. As such it is fallible and also, by extension, cannot be proved. The usual vehicle for developing this capacity is social interaction, and the autistic person is likely to have fewer opportunities than others for experiencing and learning in this interactive way.

This links to Frith's concept of 'central coherence' in that one of the main precursors to the development of a theory of mind is the development of joint attention, in which (for example) infant and caregiver look together at an object of interest. This kind of seeing is necessarily focused rather than scattered. The attainment of a theory of mind – and the same can hold for empathy – depends on an understanding of the mind as the metaphoric 'engine-room' of representation, including the production of beliefs and categories of feeling.

People on the autistic spectrum seem to share the experience of feeling unprotected by relationships. Compensatory – or over-compensatory – rituals and structures take the place of relational bonds in creating a feeling of safety in the world. Again, it would be a misconception to assume that people with autism are cold and unemotional. They can have and express strong experiences of anger, sadness and grief; it may even be said that the autist's affective world is characterised by surfeit rather than scarcity of emotion. There might be difficulties in understanding more subtle shades of feeling or those based on belief (surprise or jealousy, for instance), where an imaginative leap into the mind of the other is needed. People on the autistic spectrum may also struggle with the appropriate or conventional expression of emotion in a social context (like at a funeral).

Art therapy and autism: psychodynamic approaches

During the 1990s psychotherapists in London were working together at the Tavistock Autism Workshop to develop post-Kleinian psychoanalytic theory and practice in response to the disorder of autism, the accompanying developmental delay and personality defences of the children they were treating. Their approach was both psychoanalytic and developmental, anchored in the analytic triad of the reliability and consistency of the setting, the transference and the countertransference. They took lack of emotional relatedness to be the core symptom (not cause) of autism, and saw the therapeutic task to be one of drawing the child into relatedness, with the therapist in the first instance as a precursor to more generalised relating to others. Usually the child was seen three times a week, with work also being offered to the parents by another therapist in the team. A significant collection of their findings was published (Alvarez and Reid, 1999) using narrative descriptions of the work in order to convey the unique problem and individual personality of each autistic child.

Art therapy works on a different basis, taking the triad of client–therapist–art-making as its core structuring principle. The art therapy approach focuses on development of creative and aesthetic as well as relational capacities, particularly as there are questions about the availability of transference phenomena in the autistic person where developmental delay pertains. The prevailing model in the 1990s for art therapists was informed by psychoanalytic theories, applied in a (usually) once weekly, non-directive process held in the predictable frame of regular session times and consistent conditions. As there is a broad-ranging pluralism of bodies of psychoanalytic theory that attempt to articulate the workings of the unconscious mind, the psychodynamic orientation has myriad applications in practice. Consequently, the papers collected in this book are deeply individual, although we do draw upon some common therapeutic structuring principles. Most notably, we made use of our own countertransference experiences within the non-directive process.

The non-directive process means that we make ourselves, the art materials and the time and space of the sessions available to the client, and, within reason, we create the conditions for them to take the lead and initiate activities, interactions and communications. Our task is openly to facilitate this process and then to try to make sense of what happens and respond in a useful and enabling way, which will be different for each person. With some the focus will be on enhancing communication, with others it may be on supporting expressive and communicative capacities, or enabling the development of creativity and relational confidence. It is often a combination of some or all of these.

Rather than being concerned with structural categories of difficulties (the triad of impairments), art therapists are more involved with the creative potentials of the individual person, focusing attention on the development of the capacities that a person has or can come to have. We try to meet and make connections with the individual, rather than having a pre-conceived notion of a goal or performance indicator of changed behaviour that we want the person to reach (as would be expected from a cognitive behavioural therapy or solution-focused approach, or from the traditional educational curriculum). We have the chance to look for meaning in apparently irrational, unnecessary and incomprehensible behaviours and rituals, rather than seeking to manage and control them.

Transference and countertransference

There is frequent reference in this book to the phenomenon of *countertransference*. Many of the contributors report challenging features of the countertransference: feeling bereft, worn down, de-skilled, unable to think (Ashby, Goldsmith, Jones). At the same time countertransference responses are valued as a way of making relational contact, and failures in this area are one of the chief difficulties for the person with autism.

Transference is the psychoanalytic term for the phenomenon whereby the patient transfers onto or endows his therapist with attributes that really belong to previous figures in the patient's history, and his earlier infantile states and modes of experience; this is not a conscious process of remembering but an unconscious one of re-enactment.

Countertransference describes the therapist's own unconscious conflicts, activated in response to the patient's transference, and can be experienced by the therapist as disturbing. Freud developed his understanding of the transference phenomenon through his work with neurotic patients and although he recognised transference as a valuable aid in his work he was not positive about countertransference, seeing it as a disruptive aspect of analysis that should be overcome. However, it has received increasing attention since Freud's time partly due to the expansion of psychoanalysis into other areas, e.g. child psychotherapy, and also because therapy is now seen much more in terms of the *relationship* between therapist and patient and the intersubjective quality of that relationship. Laplanche and Pontalis say that there is considerable disagreement in psychoanalysis regarding the extent to which countertransference can be applied but one technique they describe resonates with the nature of the countertransference experiences described in this book: 'To allow oneself to be guided by one's own countertransference reactions, which in this perspective are often not distinguished from emotions felt' (Laplanche and Pontalis, 1998: 93).

Jung was in agreement with Freud on the therapeutic value of transference but differed on countertransference; whereas Freud saw it as an unwelcome intrusion, Jung, while aware of the dangers of becoming drawn into an unhelpful identification with the patient, saw the potential value of the countertransference. 'You can exert no influence if you are not susceptible to influence ... The patient influences (the analyst) unconsciously ... One of the best known symptoms of this is the countertransference evoked by the transference' (Jung, 1929 in Perry, 1998: 142). It was Jung's awareness of the anti-therapeutic potential of the countertransference that led him, like Freud, to insist on a rigorous process of training and analysis for prospective analysts, believing that analysts can only accompany their patients as far as they themselves had gone in the process of self-realisation. Perry, while acknowledging the importance of a training analysis, suggests that this is no longer a valid standpoint, arguing that it is possible to work with victims of catastrophes without having experienced the same catastrophe. 'What is important is that the analyst can be in touch with and relate to his/her own internal persecutor/ victim complex' (Perry, 1998: 157).

We should therefore be wary of claiming that the countertransference can lead us to an understanding of what it is like to be autistic; at best it might give us an experience of how autism expresses itself *in relationship*. If we have recognisable feeling responses to the autistic person, it is likely that others will also. However, the therapist – by virtue of her training, experience and the boundaries of the therapeutic situation – tries to bear these feelings in order to sustain and reach an understanding of the affective connection, while others in settings with different demands might firstly react or try to manage behaviour.

Within the non-directive framework with the autistic person in particular, the therapist is likely to make substantial use of their own felt responses. Indeed for large amounts of time it can seem that this is all we have got to go on, when the autistic person appears to be unavailable in the more usual ways we would expect in the art therapy context (not making art work, images, nor talking, nor making relational attachments). Fundamentally, countertransference refers to a particular component of all human interaction that we hone and develop into a therapeutic tool. It involves becoming more and more mindful and attuned to the specific responses evoked in ourselves in the therapy situation. This may be in the form of distinctive physical or sensory responses (overwhelming fatigue, match-stick eyes, pains and other bodily sensations), unexpected or surprising thoughts or images coming to mind when we are trying to concentrate on the situation and person before us, or associations we make to particular aspects of the material or experience within the therapeutic situation.

Working in this way puts us in a privileged position, dependent on structuring principles – like a regular session, lasting a set amount of time – which can be challenged by other professionals, whose priority might be the management of autistic behaviours (see Ashby's chapter). However, the non-directive stance enables the psychodynamic practitioner better to identify the unconscious impact of the other than would be possible if they were with the person for longer periods in an more ordinary way.

The use of art materials

Art therapists' clinical training builds upon their personal knowledge and experience of visual and creative expression in two and three dimensions, and through performance. However, unlike art, art therapy is not produced with reference to the wider public arena, but instead is held by a frame of structural and psychological boundaries. This space can be created in unpromising situations (like open wards in a hospital) as well as in a designated art room. Likewise, materials may be traditional art media but can also include found objects and features of the therapy room; for example, a piece of cellophane (Goldsmith's chapter) or water running from a tap (Byers, Ginsberg). Art materials and processes are bound up with our professional identity, and in offering them to our clients we may feel as if we are offering something valuable of ourselves. Some of the accounts in this book describe the difficult feelings engendered in the therapist when this offering is refused.

It is the *potential* rather than the physical substance of the materials that is important. In a sense, they are a kind of embodiment of Winnicott's 'potential space'; an intermediary substance offering possibilities for communication, play and creative development. (This may be why his work frequently appeals to art therapists). Yet, as we shall see in the case accounts gathered here, this 'third area' is often not available in the usual way in work with autistic individuals for reasons to do with the capacity to use symbols. When symbolism (and an opportunity for shared meaning) seems evident to the therapist, it can be denied by the autistic client (see Moore's chapter); the identification with the image that one might usually expect is not forthcoming. Jung conceived of the artist as one able to transform his or her 'prime material' into something beyond mere reproduction or representation; he proposed a *transcendent function* for symbolic activity, through which the tension between inner and outer worlds can be held (Jung, 1916: para. 166–8). In Goldsmith's study, we shall see that it can be hard to achieve this transformation.

Nevertheless, in work with people with autism, whose reference points may lie largely in the realm of the concrete, the particular, the use of art materials can provide a tangible focus. Potentially, they can also deflect the 'interpersonal glare' that autistic people can struggle with, giving the opportunity for a 'holding pattern' of repetitive or ritualistic activity to dilute the intensity of the situation. Where verbal communications might be hard to understand, interactions with and through the materials give the therapist a wider, more flexible interpretative palette and broader field for engagement. Art products can endure from session to session and can be a focus of joint reflection, as well as physical evidence of the continuity of the therapeutic relationship.

Perspectives on autism from psychoanalysis

In 1930 – predating Kanner – Klein wrote a paper entitled, 'The Importance of Symbol Formation in the Development of the Ego', resulting from her work with a boy who she describes as having 'an unusual inhibition of ego development' (Klein, 1930: 26). Today her boy patient, 'Dick', would almost certainly be described as autistic; he is portrayed as lacking in affect and uninterested in making emotional connections with others. His speech was poorly developed and he was unable to play in the usual way.

In the 1960s, Bruno Bettelheim presented a series of case studies of children he described as autistic, emphasising their fearful nature and vulnerability (Bettelheim, 1967). Influenced by his experiences in a Nazi concentration camp, he argued that autistic presentations are 'psychogenic' in origin, the result of trauma or (in the case of infantile autism) hostility from the parents. His work has been the subject of controversy, partly because he elaborated the idea that inadequate parenting, especially on the part of the mother, causes autism, and partly because of allegations of abuse and fabrication made about him and his work. Although Bettleheim's work has been discredited in some respects, his analysis of the art work produced by the children he described may still be of interest to art therapists today.

The psychoanalytic accounts of autism by Donald Meltzer *et al.* (1975) emphasise deficits in the development of abstract thought and an absence of psychic coherence, where perception is not integrated and is experienced as isolated sensory events. He describes the autistic child as lost in unthinking reverie and unavailable for communication, so that links are 'broken' and there is little or no awareness of the connections between objects and phenomena.

This insight from Meltzer parallels the tenets of Central Coherence Theory and accounts for the autistic child's difficulty with continuity, interrelatedness and the larger gestalts of experience. Meltzer also advises on the need for the therapist to be active on occasions and attempt to disrupt repetitive activities – 'to mobilise the suspended attention of the child in its autistic state, in order to bring it back into transference contact' (Meltzer *et al.*, 1975: 15). These recommendations for active interventions on the part of the therapist are interesting in the context of this book and the responses of the authors, several of whom describe feeling moved to interact with their client through the art medium.

The work of the child psychotherapist Frances Tustin has been influential in informing psychodynamic approaches to autism. Tustin presents autism as a maladaptive response to a catastrophic awareness of bodily separateness in early infancy, before the baby has the psychic resources to deal with it. Distancing herself from notions of poor parenting, she suggests that there may be a neurobiological predisposition to this kind of developmental disruption.

Like many autism theorists, Tustin devised a system of categories reflecting the affected person's degree of withdrawal from the world (Tustin, 1981). She posits the 'encapsulated child' and the 'confusional child'. The former has virtually no connection to the world of objects and relationships, only intermittently moving in and out of his or her protective shell. The confusional child has greater potential to form attachments but finds it hard to tolerate the independent existence of the other. In both types of child, a loss of blissful union with the maternal object constellates the threat of annihilation.

Meltzer and Tustin influenced Ogden, who says, 'When infantile anxiety is extreme (for constitutional and/or environmental reasons) the system of defences', 'becomes hypertrophied and rigidified' (Ogden, 1989: 50).

On the same note as Meltzer *et al.* (1975), he refers to the newborn infant as experiencing a state of unbounded sensation. In normal development the combination of rhythmic attention and continuity of experience, often felt through the skin, enables the infant gradually to organise the sensations that flow through him. This has not been achieved by the person on the severe end of the autistic spectrum who continues to experience unbounded sensations and is unable to develop towards awareness of self and other.

Ogden was also influenced by Bick's theories. He says 'Bick (1968, 1986) uses the phrase "second skin formation" to describe the way in which the individual attempts to create a substitute for a deteriorating sense of the cohesiveness of skin surface' (1989: 70–1). Thus the autist touches or hits his body rhythmically or becomes absorbed in rigid formulations such as timetables.

Ogden notes that pathological autism develops 'for constitutional and/or environmental reasons' (1989: 50). Purely 'psychogenic' theories have been largely discredited and it is now usual to give a primary role to organic or genetic factors in determining the onset of autism. However, despite intense and extensive speculation, there is no single clear-cut cause and it is likely that a complex intertwining of neurobiological and environmental strands is at play. Our main concern here is not with aetiology but with the effect of the condition of autism.

Symbol formation

A central characteristic common to people with autistic spectrum disorders is a difficulty in drawing the raw data of contingent existence into meaningful patterns and categories (Frith, 1989). This process, which most of us take for granted, mediates between the inner world of feelings and the outer world of events and enables us to come to an understanding of the outside world that is usually facilitated in childhood through imaginative activity and symbolic play.

Symbolisation is a way of re-creating and re-presenting the world that allows the individual's experience to be shared with and validated by others. This sharing of experience is evident in our work as artists and also in the way we look at and interpret images; when we stand in front of a painting we may look for meaning or recognise something familiar in the work of the other. Similarly, the interpretation of dreams, images, phantasies and symptoms in psychoanalytic work reveals latent, unconscious symbolism. It is perhaps not surprising that as art therapists we are drawn to psychoanalytic concepts, recognising in them something of our own creative endeavours.

Several chapters in this book are informed by psychoanalytic theory from Klein and the post-Kleinian school of Object Relations; others by Contemporary Independents like Bion and Winnicott while Jung and Lacan are also represented and deserve consideration in the context of imagination and symbolic function.

Klein's 'The Importance of Symbol Formation in the Development of the Ego' (see above) was the result of her work with a boy she describes as having 'an unusual inhibition of ego development' (Klein, 1930: 26). Klein's interpretations and account of her work make uncomfortable reading in the light of our current understanding of autism. However, her work with Dick confirmed her developing understanding of symbolism and she came to the conclusion that, without the capacity to symbolise, ego development is compromised. 'Symbolism is the foundation of all sublimation and of every talent', and 'upon it is built up the subject's relation to the outside world and reality in general' (Klein, 1930: 25).

Klein described an early stage of the infant's mental development at which sadistic phantasies become active: 'The excess of sadism gives rise to anxiety and sets in motion the ego's earliest modes of defence' (Klein, 1930: 25). The anxiety generated by these sadistic impulses and fear of retaliation from the objects attacked in phantasy give rise to an early form of symbolic activity. The infant moves from crude equivalences, formed through the mechanism of identification, to an ability to tolerate feelings of loss, ambiguity and ambivalence (the so-called 'depressive position'). For individuals with autism, this normative sequence does not seem to have progressed smoothly. As a result, the atmosphere in the therapy room often seems impregnated with very early developmental states.

Segal developed Klein's concept of symbolic equation, making a clear distinction between it and the 'symbol proper' which she described as 'being available for sublimation ... its own characteristics are recognized, respected and used. The symbol is used not to deny but overcome loss' (Segal, 1988: 57). The symbolic equation, however, belongs to earlier stages of development; it is experienced more concretely and is felt to be the original object. This is illustrated in Chapter 4 when Wilson's client 'cuts Mary in half'.

In the absence of a fully fledged symbolic vocabulary, some typical autistic features can be seen as attempts to manage loss or to master experience through, for example, an extreme attachment to sameness and to non-functional routines.

Whatever the aetiology, all the experiences described in this book are consistent with disturbances in symbol formation or a 'symbolic attitude', for instance: a shutting down of the 'potential space' (Dolphin, Goldsmith); a very 'concrete' use of materials with symbolic potential (Ginsberg, Wilson); problems with mobilising thinking (Goldsmith, Ashby, Dolphin). The path towards shared meaning may be vexed and challenging.

Art therapy and autism: the literature to 2000

In 1994 Tipple described the prevailing practice in art therapy and learning disabilities during the 1980s as being characterised by a reluctance to use 'interpretation' with this client group. In this paper he suggests that some art therapists can be very wary of interpretation, perhaps being protective of the 'deeply metaphoric' nature of the artwork (MacLagen, 1989) or wary of misinterpretation (Case and Dalley, 1992). He describes Schaverien's (1992) statement that stages of 'identification', 'familiarisation' and 'acknowledgement' have to have taken place before 'interpretations can help', suggesting that learning disabled clients in individual sessions are not likely to achieve all of Schaverien's stages.

Tipple describes a session in which he did a drawing with his client followed by an interpretation about the pain of loss (Tipple, 1994: 34). It clearly brought some relief and understanding for his client but he also acknowledges that a 'common sense' and flexible approach is needed. He suggests that interpretations are made with 'a more communicative style' (1994: 32), which includes 'the communication of understanding and the sharing of insights' (1994: 32).

It seems that interpretation was more evident in art therapy practice in the following decade; in 1998 both Stack and Fox record using it as part of their approach. Indeed it is used in much of the work recorded in this book; for example, Dolphin, Ginsberg, Byers, Jones and Moore all describe naming what feelings their clients' behaviours might be communicating, whilst Wilson describes a well-timed interpretation that causes a positive change in a group member's mood.

Publications in 1998 returned to the significance of the art in art therapy. Stack points out that the client can 'move in and out of his shell by interacting with me in the first part of each session then subsequently retreating' (Stack, 1998: 107) into his repetitive images. Evans (1998) shows how social interaction is less fraught for the child on the autistic spectrum if it takes place within the art process. However, Fox points out that behaviour itself can be symbolic and that the art therapist should take this into account as well.

Both Fox and Stack recommend long-term art therapy for autistic clients, Fox suggesting that there is the possibility of change over time. Many of the case studies in this volume describe work that took place over several years (Byers, Goldsmith, Ashby, Jones).

Also in 1998, Evans and Rutten-Saris point our attention to the work of Stern (1985), saying that 'while an object-relations approach informs practice, alternative methodologies are also necessary' for art therapy with children in the autistic spectrum. They describe Stern's theories about 'the perceptive and communicative process that, at the level of pre-verbal experience, provide the sensory foundations for such' (1998: 57–9), theories that were developed from Stern's observations of very young infants. Stern, being both a developmental psychologist and a psychoanalyst, clarifies the distinction between the two approaches these different disciplines have to infancy by describing the infant of developmental psychology as an '*observed infant*' and that of psychoanalysis as a '*clinical infant*'. The observed infant's behaviour, e.g. hand–eye coordination, the ability to smile, etc., is examined at the time of its occurrence. He describes the clinical infant as a reconstruction, the product of two people, the therapist and the patient. He considers both these approaches indispensable for understanding the development of the infant's sense of self. 'The clinical infant breathes subjective life into the observed infant, while the observed infant points towards the general theories upon which one can build the inferred subjective life of the clinical infant' (Stern, 1998: 14).

The developmental account described by Stern is one in which 'new senses of the self serve as organising principles of development' (Stern, 1998: 19). He says his ideas are closest in psychoanalytic terms to those of Mahler and Klein because the central concern of both theirs and his theory is the infant's experience of self and other. However, he thinks they differ in the nature of the experience, the order in which developmental sequences occur and in the fact that Stern's conceptual self is not confused with or dependent on the development of Freud's concepts of the *ego* and the *id.* It's possible to see some common ground between Stern's ideas and those of Fordham who developed Jung's concept of the self, suggesting it was present from birth as an organising principle of integration.

The case studies: art therapy at work

The main body of the book – subdivided thematically – provides examples of art therapy practice with people on the autistic spectrum, reflecting a range of age groups, clinical presentations, settings and approaches. All the authors have used pseudonyms to protect the identity of their clients.

The blank page: art therapy without the art

In Chapter 2, Matt Dolphin introduces some core themes of the book in his description of an art therapy assessment with a man with Asperger's Syndrome ('Michael'), an encounter characterised by paralysed communication. Michael's inability or unwillingness to use art materials in the sessions found an acoustic counterpoint in his silence or barely audible words. The author considers how this apparent resistance might have resulted from both the petrifying effects of bereavement and factors associated with autistic spectrum conditions. A desire for pre-linguistic symbiosis seemed to exist alongside a grinding antagonism between client and therapist. Dolphin frankly acknowledges his own inertia in this situation and the perceived threat to his competence. However, movement (and imagery) entered the sessions in a surprising fashion and – though the ending remains unresolved – there was a hope of the work resonating for both client and therapist.

Sticking with it: holding the therapeutic process

The next three chapters bring distinctive voices to the theme of 'holding', an oft-used, polyvalent and sometimes nebulous term in writing on therapy. Holding emerges as a process that takes place on different levels, achieved through various mechanisms and therapeutic attitudes.

Sue Ginsberg reprises the theme of emptiness and silence in her account of art therapy with a young boy ('Peter') with very little language; the sessions took place in a primary school for children with moderate learning difficulties. Ginsberg describes the difficulty of providing safety and regulation without colluding in the client's desire for a totally predictable world. Peter's dread of absence and need to fill every space – material or psychological – seemed to relate to a fragile sense of psychic coherence. The theme of gaps was given additional prominence by the particular rhythm of the academic year. However, the work was moved forward by a process of enactment through the space and materials that, in combination with the therapist's responses, is seen to have a kind of quasi-symbolic function.

In the following chapter, Penelope Wilson presents an art therapy group of five autistic people aged between 20 and 30, with an art therapist and art therapy trainee (the author) as co-facilitators. Wilson argues for the effectiveness of this working model, noting the extra practical and emotional support available to clients and the value of two perspectives when the co-therapists reflect upon the work together. If the group's 'parents' were able to maintain clear boundaries and a consistency of time and place, group members had the potential to achieve greater spontaneity; there was enough structure to satisfy the autistic person's need for routine without rigidity. Sessions are described as having a lively and chaotic atmosphere, held together by the therapists' attention to emerging interpersonal dynamics and to individuals who needed extra support to participate in the group.

The preoccupation with gaps and breaks in continuity noted by Ginsberg is also a feature of Angela Byers' long-term work with an autistic man (Chapter 5). The author introduces 'Christopher', describing his love of flow and exploring edges, as well as his responses to her own interventions, which she calls a form of 'reflecting out loud'. Byers' understanding of Christopher's behaviour was influenced by Ogden's concept of the 'autistic contiguous position' (Ogden, 1989) and how disturbances at this stage of development can play a role in later presentations of autism. She also draws upon Ogden's later paper 'On Holding and Containing, Being and Dreaming' (2004), which considers Winnicott's emphasis on time and rhythm in the day-to-day handling of the infant, as well as Bion's description of the origins of thinking in the 'containment' within the caregiver's responsiveness. Theoretical thinking itself – as well as the actual ideas – emerges as a structuring principle, enabling Byers to create a framework for understanding and to provide an experience of containment for the client.

New perspectives: steps away from the norm

Chapters 6 and 7 present examples of work that depart from the 'orthodox' model of art therapy as a process unfolding between client and therapist in a dedicated art room. Alison Goldsmith brings a post-Jungian perspective to her account of art therapy with 'Margaret', a woman in her fifties. The setting was a residential care home and the scope and limitations of working in such circumstances are described. The role of imagination, especially that of the therapist, and the possibility that trauma may cast a strong shadow over work with a client who has been in long-term institutional care are central to the chapter. Goldsmith considers Jung's concept of the symbolic, and how both conventional art materials and 'found' objects began to transcend their raw physicality in her work with Margaret, whose image-making tended to be repetitive and descriptive.

Elizabeth Ashby also takes us into a setting in which it was difficult to maintain therapeutic boundaries: a day unit for people with profound and complex learning disabilities whose behaviour could be chaotic and hard to manage. Service users' difficulties with communication and understanding boundaries were compounded by structural problems within the institution. The author describes how her foundering attempts to engage a highly active young man ('Colin') were bolstered by the development of sessions facilitated by both herself and a music therapist: a different kind of joint working to the more established model described earlier by Wilson (Chapter 4). The new collaboration furnished a renewed energy and sense of safety, and a fertile sharing of skills; the co-facilitator's perspective also revealed progress that the therapist alone had found it hard to perceive. The male–female pairing seemed to represent a positive parental dyad for Colin, while the cross-disciplinary partnership engendered fresh approaches to the work.

New growth: facilitating development through art therapy

In Chapter 8, Ruth Jones shares some of the questions, themes and challenges that emerged through the course of four years' art therapy with 'Elizabeth', who was 5½ when offered weekly sessions in her school for children with moderate learning difficulties. In early sessions, Elizabeth's determined production of highly controlled and repetitive schemas, and the affective paralysis experienced by the author, challenged her stamina and sense of effectiveness. In an echo of Chapter 2, there were lengthy periods of 'non-art' time. In this case, however, the latter is recognised as a stage towards letting go of personal rituals and moving towards a more spontaneous, exploratory style of expression. Finally, with the support of the therapist's attentive availability, Elizabeth was able to produce art work that seemed to carry a fully symbolic intent.

In the final case study, Lesley Anne Moore gives her account of six months' individual art therapy with a young man ('Simon') who displayed autistic features but without a formal diagnosis of his condition. The author explores the potential overlap between autism and mental illness; the clinical presentation centred around Simon's reluctance to eat, and his belief that people might have been able to intrude upon his private thoughts if he took food into his body. In an interesting parallel to Goldsmith's chapter, there is a question as to whether Simon was actually autistic or if his symptoms were an expression of his profound isolation. Against this background and that of his family relationships, Moore depicts Simon's tentative steps towards greater independence, and his increasing ability to explore his burgeoning adult self by making art within the supportive context of the therapeutic relationship.

The current context

Chapter 10 provides a survey of the developments in art therapy literature over the past decade. We ask whether the givens of a psychodynamic orientation are still valid. Much of the work we present and reflect upon has produced outcomes that still stand up to scrutiny, in many cases prefiguring more recent approaches.

We explore the tension between diagnosis and 'personhood', with the need to acknowledge diagnostic categories and pitch therapeutic intervention accordingly, without losing sight of the individual concerned. The concluding section of the book considers how the experiences, themes and theoretical stances explored thus far might inform practice both now and in the future.

References

Alvarez, A. and Reid, S. (eds) (1999) *Autism and Personality: Findings from the Tavistock Autism Workshop*, London: Routledge.

American Psychiatric Association (1980) *Diagnostic and Statistical Manual of Mental Disorders (DSM-III)*, 3rd edition, Washington: American Psychiatric Association.

—— (1994) *Diagnostic and Statistical Manual of Mental Disorders (DSM-IV)*, 4th edition, Washington: American Psychiatric Association.

Asperger, H. (1944) 'Die Autistischen Psychopathen im Kindesalter', *Archiv fur Psychiatrie und Nervenkrakheiten*, 177: 76–136.

Attwood, T. (2003) 'Is there a difference between Asperger's Syndrome and high functioning autism?' Online. Available at: www.sacramentoasis.com/docs/8-22-03/as_&_hfa.pdf (accessed 17 October 2012).

Baron-Cohen, S., Leslie, A. and Frith, U. (1985) 'Does the autistic child have a "theory of mind"?', *Cognition*, 21 (1): 37–46.

Bettelheim, B. (1967) *The Empty Fortress: Infantile Autism and the Birth of the Self*, New York: Free Press.

Bion, W. (1962, reprinted edition 1984) *Learning from Experience*, London: Karnac (Books) Ltd.

Bleuler, E. (1908, translated 1987) 'The prognosis of dementia praecox: the group of schizophrenias' in Cutting, J. and Shepherd, M. (eds), *The Clinical Roots of the Schizophrenia Concept*, Cambridge: Cambridge University Press.

Bragge, A. and Fenner, P. (2009) 'The emergence of the "Interactive Square" as an approach to art therapy with children on the autistic spectrum', *International Journal of Art Therapy*, 14 (1): 17–28.

Case, C. and Dalley, T. (1992) *The Handbook of Art Therapy*, London: Routledge.

Evans, K. (1998) 'Sharing experience and sharing meaning: art therapy for children with autism', *Journal of the British Association of Art Therapists*, 3 (1): 17–25.

Evans, K. and Rutten-Saris, M. (1998) 'Shaping vitality affects, enriching communication: art therapy for children with autism' in Sandle, D. (ed.), *Development and Diversity: New Applications in Art Therapy*, London and New York: Free Association Books.

Evans, K. and Dubowski, J. (2001) *Art Therapy with Children on the Autistic Spectrum: Beyond Words*, London and Philadelphia: Elizabeth Kingsley Publishers.

Fox, L. (1998) 'Lost in space: the relevance of art with clients who have autism or autistic features' in Rees, M. (ed.), *Drawing on Difference: Art Therapy with People Who Have Learning Difficulties*, London and New York: Routledge.

Frith, U. (1989) *Autism: Explaining the Enigma*, Oxford: Blackwell.

Galan, C. (2012) 'Proposed DSM-V criteria for autism sparks debate'. Online. Available at: http://beta.in-mind.org/social-psychology-headlines/proposed-dsm-v-criteria-autism-sparks-debate (accessed 20 October 2012).

Gardner, H. (1985) *Frames of the Mind: The Theory of Multiple Intelligences*, London: Paladin.

Henley, D. (2001) 'Annihilation anxiety and fantasy in the art of children with Asperger's Syndrome and others on the autistic spectrum', *American Journal of Art Therapy*, 39 (4): 113–21.

Jackson, M. (director) (2010) 'Temple Grandin'. TV Movie, released 6 February 2010, distributed by HBO.

Jung, C.G. (1916) 'The transcendent function', *Collected Works 8*, London: Routledge.

Kanner, L. (1943) 'Autistic disturbances of affective contact', *Nervous Child*, 2: 217–50.

Kellerman, J. (2001) *Autism, Art and Children: The Stories We Draw*, Wesport, Connecticut and London: Bergin and Garvey.

Klein, M. (1930) 'The importance of symbol-formation in the development of the ego', *International Journal of Psycho-Analysis*, 10 (1): 24–39.

Laplanche, J. and Pontalis, J.B. (1988) *The Language of Psychoanalysis*, London: Karnac.

MacLagen, D. (1989) 'The aesthetic dimension in art: luxury or necessity?', *Journal of the British Association of Art Therapists*, Spring: 10–13.

Meltzer, D., Bremner, J., Hoxter, S., Weddell, D. and Wittenberg, I. (1975) *Explorations in Autism: A Psychoanalytic Study*, Strath Tay: Clunie Press.

Meyeritz-Katz, J. (2008) '"Other people have a secret that I do not know": art psychotherapy in private practice with an adolescent girl with Asperger's Syndrome' in Case, C. and Dalley, T. (eds), *Art Therapy with Children from Infancy to Adolescence*, London and New York: Routledge.

Ogden, T. (1989, reprinted edition 1992) *The Primitive Edge of Experience*, London: Karnac.

Ogden, T.H. (2004) 'On holding and containing, being and dreaming', *International Journal of Psycho-analysis*, 85: 1349–64.

Patterson, Z. (2008) 'From "Beanie" to "Boy"' in Case, C. and Dalley, T. (eds), *Art Therapy with Children from Infancy to Adolescence*, London and New York: Routledge.

Perry, C. (1998) 'Transference and countertransference', in Young-Eisendrath, P. and Dawson, T. (eds), *The Cambridge Companion to Jung*, Cambridge: Cambridge University Press.

Rostron, J. (2010) 'On amodal perception and language in art therapy with autism', *International Journal of Art Therapy*, 15 (1): 36–49.

Rutter, M. (1978) 'Diagnosis and definition of childhood autism', *Journal of Autism and Developmental Disorders*, 8 (2): 139–61.

Sacks, O. (1995) *An Anthropologist on Mars*, London: Picador.

Schaverien, J. (1992) *The Revealing Image: Analytic Art Psychotherapy in Theory and Practice*, London and New York: Tavistock/Routledge.

Segal, H. (1988) *The Work of Hanna Segal*, London: Free Association Books.

Skaife, S. (2001) 'Making visible: art therapy and intersubjectivity', *Journal of the British Association of Art Therapists*, 6 (2): 40–50.

Stack, M. (1998) 'Humpty Dumpty's shell: working with autistic defence mechanisms in art therapy' in Rees, M. (ed.), *Drawing on Difference: Art Therapy with People who have Learning Difficulties*, London and New York: Routledge.

Stern, D. (1985) *The Interpersonal World of the Infant: A View from Psychoanalysis and Developmental Psychology*, New York: Basic Books.

—— (1998) *The Interpersonal World of the Infant: A View from Psychoanalysis and Developmental Psychology*, 2nd edition, London: Karnac Books.

Symington, N. (1986) *The Analytic Experience*, New York: St. Martin's Press.

Tipple, R. (1994) 'Communication and interpretation in art therapy with people who have a learning disability', *Inscape: The Journal of the British Association of Art Therapists*, 2: 31–5.

—— (2008) 'Paranoia and paracosms: brief art therapy with a youngster with Asperger's Syndrome' in Case, C. and Dalley, T. (eds), *Art Therapy with Children from Infancy to Adolescence*, London and New York: Routledge.

Tustin, F. (1981, revised edition 1992) *Autistic States in Children*, London and New York: Routledge.

Volkmar, F. (1998) 'Categorical approaches to the diagnosis of autism: an overview of DSM-IV and ICD-10', *Autism* 2: 45–59.

Williams, D. (1998) *Autism and Sensing: The Unlost Instinct*, London and Philadelphia: Jessica Kingsley.

Wing, L. (1981) 'Language, social and cognitive impairments in autism and severe mental retardation', *Journal of Autism and Developmental Disorders*, 11 (1): 31–4.

Wing, L. and Gould, J. (1978) 'Systematic recording of behaviors and skills of retarded and psychotic children', *Journal of Autism and Developmental Disorders*, 8 (1): 79–97.

Wing, L. and Attwood, A. (1987) 'Syndromes of autism and atypical development' in Cohen, D.J. and Donnelan, A. (eds), *Handbook of Autism*, New York: Wiley.

Winnicott, D. (1965, reprinted edition 1990) *The Maturational Processes and the Facilitating Environment*, London: Karnac.

World Health Organization (1992) *International Statistical Classification of Diseases and Related Health Problems*, Geneva: WHO.

Chapter 2

Frozen in headlights

Working with loss in art therapy with a man with Asperger's Syndrome

Matt Dolphin

The following chapter, based on an experience from clinical training, centres on a six-session art therapy assessment with 'Michael' (a pseudonym), a 33-year-old man with Asperger's Syndrome. The work described made a deep impression on me, yet was characterised by non-activity: few words, less movement, no art work. If the reader is disappointed by the lack of images accompanying this piece, this will, I feel, resonate with my dismay at the absence of art making in the sessions. As for the affective quality of the therapy, it appeared that emotional energy – especially connected to loss and change – was frightening to Michael, feelings often seeming obscured, cut off, deadened or frozen.

My motives for writing about this particular experience are related to the concept of 'internalisation', as described by David Edwards in his article on *Endings*: 'the process of making sense of the experience and attempting to make good use of it' (Edwards, 1997: 49). Internalisation – like the grieving process – is helped by the use of symbolic objects (such as a piece of writing), which reconcile inner and outer worlds and, in this case, may also hold a symbolic space for a client who would have difficulty doing this for himself.

The intensity of the encounter led me to an in-depth examination of my feelings towards Michael, of my own resistance to therapeutic involvement and my struggle with a countertransference that often had me in its grip. The absence of any apparent response to the therapist, be it artistic, verbal or kinetic, presents a challenge to faith and ability.

Asperger's Syndrome: the clinical picture and some implications for art therapy

There is general agreement that AS (a common abbreviation) features 'no clinically significant delay in cognitive development' (DSM-IV – American Psychiatric Association 1994). Nevertheless, it would appear that some developmental stages have been negotiated differently, so that there is an uneven profile of intellectual and emotional abilities; the characteristic triad of autistic symptomatology is present. Mastery of experience through ritualised control is marked, a feature intensified at times of stress and transition; this was particularly relevant to Michael.

Ritualised behaviour is compounded by an all-consuming preoccupation with a rigidly circumscribed special interest or area of expertise; Michael was said to be 'obsessed' with buses and trams (as well as with frequent ablutions). The special interest may dominate imaginative and intellectual activity, often serving to prevent the involvement of others. An 'alternative script' (Attwood, 1998: 30) may be avoided because of difficulties conceptualising the thoughts of others. An impaired 'theory of mind', together with a lack of intuitive feel for the rhythm and tempo of social reciprocity, can come across as an absence of empathy. Partial insight into these problems may lead to depression.

A final note on the quality of speech: I had heard that the verbal output of people with Asperger's Syndrome tends to be intrusive, one-sided and overwhelming, used to repel or entangle rather than to communicate. Michael, on the other hand, was a selective mute, a flipside that nonetheless had a similar effect: the paralysis of communicative exchange. Selective mutism is a communication disorder in which people are unable to speak in particular situations that they find stressful or hard to understand (for example, some individuals with higher-functioning autism in certain social settings). (Originally I used the older term 'elective mute', out of favour since 1994 but perhaps reflective of my frustrations in working with Michael).

Signposts to countertransference

Psychology-based literature refers to the contradictory feelings that these clients can arouse. They are frequently described as naive and eccentric, qualities that 'evoke the maternal or predatory instinct in others' (Attwood, 1998: 161). On the other hand, they can be perceived as manipulative, possessing 'a surprising capacity for anti-social behaviour' (Tantam, 1992).

In his original description, Asperger pointed out that 'a dash of autism' – the ability to withdraw into a complex inner world – is a prerequisite to success in science and the arts. The idea of autism as a seamless continuum suggests that there are diagnostic grey areas as we progress along it, between AS and the normal range. Working with autistic clients can crystallise those parts of the practitioner that oscillate between chaos and a compensatory drive towards coherence.

The question of resistance

As Cundall (1991) points out, the term 'resistance' (in contrast to 'defence') implies the presence of an impetus towards change and insight, which (for a number of reasons) the client – or therapist – finds it hard to respond to. However, it is important to recognise that the forces holding back change may be due to neurobiological as well as psychodynamic factors.

Resistance to therapeutic engagement can also be a feature of the therapist's attitude, especially in the face of a very quiet or passive client: 'These patients can stir up strong resistance in the therapist, because of the threat they pose to our competence' (Cundall, 1991: 18).

The setting

The art therapy department was part of a Therapeutic Core Unit for people with learning disabilities, some with superimposed mental ill health manifesting as challenging behaviour. The unit offered an array of therapies and clinical approaches: art and music therapy, psychology, speech therapy, social education, psychiatry, behavioural intervention. Michael came to the Core Unit with an escort from his home in the community, one afternoon a week.

Art therapy aims and approaches

The unit was extremely well equipped to offer art therapy. The department enjoyed the use of a light, spacious art room, brim-full of materials and displays of finished creations and works-in-progress. An adjoining office/storage area had tea and coffee making facilities. To me, the overall impression was of a fertile and welcoming atmosphere; perhaps, to clients like Michael, the wide choice of equipment could be intimidating.

As Lesley Fox notes (1998: 74), a degree of scepticism surrounds psychodynamic modes of intervention in relation to clients with autistic features (in contrast to, say, Applied Behaviour Analysis). Psychiatrists Ami Klin and Fred Volkmar believe that 'supportive psychotherapy focused on problems of empathy, social difficulties and depressive symptoms may be helpful, although it is usually very difficult for individuals with AS to engage in more intensive insight-oriented psychotherapy' (1995: 13).

Perhaps I took doubts about a psychodynamic approach – together with no fully formed ideas of possible alternative strategies – into the work with Michael. There was also no question of using the image as a tool for communication, for we were together, for the most part, at a pre-representational stage, negotiating a way to share the same space.

Background and referral

The consultant referred Michael because she found him angry and frustrated about living away from his mother. While living in the family home, he had apparently been aggressive towards his mum when his rituals were interfered with. His 'obsessional' behaviour was linked to the diagnosis of Asperger's Syndrome.

Further information was obtained from the community nurse to whom Michael had also been referred. He had been sharing a private residential home with three other clients for about six months, and now seemed quite settled after finding the initial move upsetting – episodes of absconding had ceased.

The changes in living accommodation had been precipitated by the death of Michael's father. Not mentioned on the referral form, this is an instance of how, particularly in the field of learning disability, one loss can lead to further losses, compounding grief with feelings of instability and helplessness. Moreover,

Michael's mother was in the process of moving out of the area. He appeared to be coping well with this added change, and would be supported to visit his mum once a month.

Nevertheless, this amounted to a considerable complex of loss and transition, and a potential undermining of Michael's main sphere of influence; his community nurse and consultant considered that he had controlled his parents' lives through his ritualistic behaviour. Beyond this the history was sketchy, particularly concerning Michael's childhood, adolescence and family relationships (especially with his father). Thus armed, I went into our initial chunk of time together, the first of a series of six assessment sessions.

The first session

Many of the themes that characterised this encounter were present from the first meeting. For example, the issue of choice: Michael knew he was coming to see the community nurse, but was unaware that he would be meeting an art therapy trainee until just before the session, in order to prevent an anticipated high level of anxiety. It could be argued that this approach merely postpones anxious feelings, potentially increasing their eventual intensity. I had also agreed to let the nurse accompany Michael into the art room and stay until he had settled; it may have felt that this was more fait accompli than reassurance. At the same time, Michael's escort remained in the reception area so that he could leave early if he wanted to. It appeared that thoughts were mixed as to whether Michael was able to make a meaningful choice to attend therapy or not.

The community nurse had a friendly, down-to-earth presence, and talked volubly about Michael's background and anxieties in new situations, while Michael sat nearby with an attitude of compliance. Then the nurse left, saying that Michael and I could now have a 'little chat', the kind of phrase people (especially parents) use when they are about to deliver a stern admonishment, or a bumbling account of the 'facts of life'.

The image of a small animal frozen by headlights entered my mind. I wasn't sure if this referred to Michael, to me or to the whole situation; probably a combination of the three. The possibility of action was nullified by a fear whose roots seemed archaic, primitive; it was as though the space was petrified, turned to stone. The image of headlights made me think of 'being in the spotlight'; perhaps Michael felt over-focused on, feared persecution by my undivided attention – especially in a one-to-one context. Stack quotes McCormack: 'The real pain was in being listened to, which is also to be thought about' (Stack, 1998: 86). Perhaps attention is enough to mobilise the spectre of this pain; Michael's response was not to say anything, thus side-stepping the possibility of being listened to.

I, on the other hand, responded to my anxiety by talking a good deal more than I usually would in the role of art therapist. However, I have little record of *what* I said; a reflection, I think, of the feeling that my words were trailing off into meaninglessness, dissolving in the ether. I do recall saying things like 'this is your space'; but therapy needs to be pitched at the right level and this statement of mine was imprecise, especially as people with Asperger's Syndrome can have problems understanding figurative speech or are prone to literal interpretation. Michael did reply to direct questions, but with a soft, indistinct tone that was very hard to hear.

Michael's body language was immensely inhibited; he held his small frame in a hunched position on the chair, his hands clasped in his lap. The slightest movement seemed a huge effort; his range of facial expression was extremely narrow and direct eye contact was impossible for him to maintain (it was replaced by the odd sidelong glance). These characteristics are all associated with AS, sometimes even to the extent of catatonia as a neurological complication. Although not present as a physiological fact, there was certainly a 'catatonic' feel to the sessions. On the other hand, I wrote of my kinaesthetic experience at the time: 'My usual body image is transformed, I swell to monstrous size and feel like an aggressive ogre'.

My attitude during this initial meeting was split between a desire to stay with these unpleasant feelings and an urge to end them by encouraging some (artistic) action. On the one hand, I aimed for an acceptance of stillness ('this is your space'); on the other, I was frustrated by Michael's lack of activity and continually tried to direct his attention towards the range of art work and image-making equipment in the room. At one point I had asked him if he wanted to try out the materials; hearing his murmured reply as a "yes", I placed an A1 sheet of white paper on the table in front of him. The paper took on huge proportions, threatening to engulf his body. Michael sat in the same position without stirring, his stasis if anything more dominant; I felt unable to provide any further direction.

As Cundall notes, there may be deep-seated inhibitions to marking a blank white surface; the act of creation is also destructive, obliterating the 'absolute' quality of emptiness in favour of an uncertain (visual) outcome (1991: 108). For some with Asperger's Syndrome, this aspect of creativity may be additionally hindered by an insistence on 'completion and perfection' (Attwood, 1998: 121). Michael may also have wondered what (artistic) expectations I had of him.

If physical motion is a problem, concrete image-making will be impossible: 'Art work cannot be made without movement and movement always produces an image – movement and image are each other's doors' (Evans and Rutten-Saris, 1996: 7). The blank page could also be seen as a visual counterpart to silence.

Sessions two and three

My supervisor suggested that this early stage of therapy might simply be about finding a way to be with someone. This felt right; but there were other ideas around too, something about Michael 'fusing' with me and trying to use me as an extension of himself, and the possibility that he was launching an attack by de-skilling me (not engaging with art materials). Indeed, looking back through my notes, I found the word 'control' cropping up four times in one short passage. I wasn't sure where the control lay though: would I be controlled if I was prompted into speaking or acting for Michael, or was I colluding in his need for time-arresting and feeling-deadening paralysis by not doing anything?

I was sure of Michael's need strictly to regulate his emotional experience. This seemed understandable, given the welter of changes and associated losses that had been visited upon him in recent months. Art therapy could have been another unwelcome new factor. Michael's extreme passivity perhaps reflected a desire for a kind of cryogenic standstill. Clients with autistic spectrum disorders can have a different sense of time: past, present and future as concepts that help us to order and cope with experiences may not be available in the same way, so that traumatic or disturbing events remain vividly in the present.

For people who have difficulties with verbal communication, it may only be possible to express feeling states by somatising them, 'acting them out' or projecting them into the environment. This is particularly relevant to the autistic continuum: 'People who are autistic often seem to make their reference points outside themselves, in concrete areas, displaying some lack in the ability to communicate within themselves on a symbolic level, so that anxiety, panic, disorientation, confusion, anger and denial are typical responses to external change' (Fox, 1998: 81). This gives useful pointers towards an intellectual understanding of Michael's contagious inertia, but such states are no easier to be with for that. Tustin's concept of 'autistic encapsulation' comes to mind: 'A freezing of life-giving properties giving propensities akin to a living death unless these tendencies can somehow be released' (Stack, 1998: 92).

I wondered how to reconcile intervention and 'allowing'. In session three I found myself staring at a plant in the art room, thinking, the plant grows of its own accord but needs feeding, watering and a fertile environment. It is probably telling that my focus was so easily distracted from the other person in the room.

Early in session two I tried to encourage Michael to use art materials through demonstration. I mentioned that he seemed to be having some difficulty trying out the pens, pencils, etc., and maybe it would be helpful if I showed him what kind of marks they made. I produced some tentative splodges with felt markers and a bit of paint, feeling much of the inhibition around 'defacing' the blank paper described earlier. I was aiming to make the marks as neutral and devoid of artistic skill as possible, but they readily transmogrified into ominous and menacing shapes, like Rorschach inkblots. My notes describe my feelings at the time as 'predatory'. Michael was perhaps communicating something to me of his vulnerability and lack of competence in this situation. A session with a relative absence of internal structure, where the emphasis is on interaction and emotional responses, can maximise the significance of Asperger's Syndrome, particularly when the client is also affected by grief and anxiety (Klin and Volkmar, 1996: 4).

My approach in the second session was also to name possible feelings in the room, with the intention of cutting through any fearful fantasies that Michael might have had about what I was thinking. I was therefore forearmed with phrases like, 'Perhaps it feels like you're not quite sure why you're here?' and, 'This may be a time when it's useful just to sit and "be" with another person'.

However, the way my process notes describe such interventions is: 'I begin babbling'. It seems that language – or the lack of a meaningful language – was an important theme in this encounter. Paul Newham's book on Therapeutic Voicework contains some interesting thoughts on silence and the softly spoken. He suggests that people who vocalise quietly can be bruised and hurt, and seek a soft voice to caress or tend to them. The mouth is a major point of exchange between an individual and the phenomenal world, receptive to sensory experience and emitting vocal or bodily material.

Phonophobia – a fear of voicing – can arise in those who fear that 'others might penetrate them and destroy their self-defence' (Newham, 1998: 81). Working with Michael, I felt both the need to establish a presence through speech and the fear that speaking was intrusive or oppressive, especially as Michael seemed unable to display any confidence with the spoken word himself. I also experienced a certain identification, remembering numerous characterisations of myself in school reports as a 'quietly determined' individual.

Newham also points up the importance of the infant's early relationship with the mother (or primary caregiver) in the development of vocalisation. The mother's facial expression provides a visual accompaniment to the acoustic message, and, 'where the mother's face is inexpressive, the baby may find it hard to mobilise its own physiognomy' (Newham, 1998: 84). In the case of an autistic child, it may be the baby who is inexpressive; nevertheless, a similar complex of physiognomic immobility, minimal eye contact and silence results.

The very need for language could be perceived as a reminder of the loss of the symbiotic relationship between mother and infant. Michael may sometimes have been functioning at a level where he expected me to know his needs and feelings without a word being spoken. Interestingly, though, he was reported to be able to talk normally to his mum; perhaps other people were perceived as more capable of breaching his defences. I never found out if he had spoken 'normally' with his father.

Spoken language having rung hollow, I spent some time consciously trying to synchronise my breathing with Michael's, inhaling and exhaling according to the (barely perceptible) rise and fall of his jacket. I had in mind the 'earthing' aim of some styles of meditation, or the kind of attunement used by Evans and Rutten-Saris: 'Breathing in the rhythm of the patient brings the art therapist and the patient into open active alertness' (1996: 17). The hypnotist might also establish rapport in this way, leading the subject to a state of openness to suggestion; but in this instance I wasn't at all sure who was hypnotising whom. The effect of breathing in time was more soporific than anything, and highlighted the difficulty of any movement beyond the involuntary motion of internal organs. Getting up to fetch something, or asking Michael if he wanted to remove his jacket, would have felt like acts of violence.

In relation to session three, I wrote: 'I have an odd feeling of being the benign yet frustrated father'. This seems an important indicator of my countertransference responses. My disappointment at the difficult course of the therapy could have carried an echo of parental disappointment at the struggle to form a relationship with a child with autistic features. From the point of view of the archetypal father, this could relate to the apparent lack of manly competence and assertiveness displayed by someone like Michael. My process notes convey the impression of a good deal of (unconscious) father-to-son type horn-locking, referring to a 'war of attrition'.

Perhaps more importantly, paternal thoughts reminded me of Michael's bereavement. Death can be frightening and confusing for those who have difficulty using symbols; for those on the autistic spectrum, the grieving process can be made harder 'by the inability to express appropriate and subtle emotions' (Attwood, 1998: 159).

Session four

Maybe, though, the sense of paralysis had too great a foothold. I felt a growing need to re-establish myself as a thinking, working art therapist, as a separately functioning entity. I voiced my concerns in a group clinical supervision, and my approach to the next session was informed, to large extent, by a suggestion from the seminar leader: to pursue my own image-making in Michael's presence, as a focus for feeling and communication (at least from my side).

This idea somewhat took me aback. I rationalised my gut inhibition as a thought that, by using the art materials myself, I would be placing myself in the role of artist, thereby removing any possibility that Michael would draw or paint. I also feared that my work(ing) could be perceived as an attack. My supervisor on placement shared some of these reservations, though maybe she also sensed my reticence. In the event strategic considerations and the possible conflicting wisdom of supervisors were irrelevant: I simply could not make an image in front of Michael.

I was still aware of the necessity of conveying my separateness in some way; my notes suggest that in fact I acted out a degree of frustration by asking a series of questions ('How are you feeling?'; 'Do you feel as if you have a choice in coming here?'), a kind of mini-interrogation. Perhaps Michael would have liked to ask me lots of questions, which he was unable to voice. In any case, there was no real shift either in me or in the atmosphere of the session. An interesting moment occurred when Michael turned to look out of the window, perhaps prompted by the sound of wind rustling in the leaves. This was more movement (besides leaving and entering the room) than I had seen from him before. I asked if something outside had caught his eye. He turned around sharply, and for a second I thought he would answer; instead he returned to his habitual posture. Maybe there was something beyond this room, this encounter, that was quite appealing.

Besides art work, something else I felt unable to do in the sessions was discuss Michael's diagnosis with him, even though it was a preoccupation of the professionals involved in his care. Writers on Asperger's Syndrome list both advantages and drawbacks of labelling. While stressing the irreducible individuality of those with AS, they point to accurate diagnostic assessment as a prerequisite to effective treatment programmes. Attwood speculates that 'the high incidence of depression in adults may be a reflection of the lack of understanding and remedial tuition that this generation experienced during childhood' (1998: 160). More pertinently, he doubts the wisdom of sharing the diagnosis with the client, suggesting this could happen 'when they are emotionally able to cope with the news' (1998: 178). With Michael, I never felt emotionally able to give it.

This, and the reluctance to paint in the sessions, may have been bound up with the question: is it possible to harm this patient? Part of me hoped my presence resonated with Michael; that I often readily colluded with his need to cut off from feeling suggests that this hope was undermined by an impression of his susceptibility to damage.

Session five

As this was the penultimate session of the assessment period, I knew that Michael and I had to begin reviewing the usefulness of the sessions together. I had a more or less ready worded spiel for this purpose, along with ideas such as joint mark making. This was perhaps exposed by ensuing events as the kind of lack of openness that can lead to 'premature closure' (Cohn, 1997: 35).

The session began in a familiar way, Michael sitting in his usual chair, usual posture. Then, with barely a pause for reflection, I reminded him of the assessment period, immediately adding: 'At this point, looking over how things have gone, do you want to continue with the sessions?' I remember Michael looking vaguely surprised and turning towards me, extremely animatedly by previous standards, as if this was the first thing I had said that actually meant anything to him. The question left little room for ambivalence, and betrayed my desire to end the uncomfortableness of contradictory feelings, to elicit a clear reaction. Michael responded with a distinct 'No'. Taken aback, I asked for clarification; again, 'No.'

My process notes reflect how unclear my thinking was at this point. After initially considering that we should see the six sessions through, I was possessed by an urge to wind things up, deciding to ask Michael if he would rather leave there and then. He said, 'Yes'. Then, as we waited for a member of the Nurses' Outreach Team to fetch him, I realised the need for concluding comments, and hastily aired some thoughts about how endings might be tinged with mixed feelings, regret and relief for example. I also said that it seemed important for Michael to make a positive choice about his life in this way. When the nurse arrived, she asked him why he wanted to finish art therapy while immediately supplying an answer in the form of a question: 'Just didn't like it?'

Once they had left I felt a little panicky; did I need to bring the assessment to an 'official' end? I even began composing letters to Michael and his house manager confirming the end of the therapy, before realising that there was the option of at least one further session if Michael wanted it.

My supervisor was away, and the music therapist (acting in her stead) came in from next door to find out how I had got on. She confirmed my growing intuition that I was being far too final, suggesting that Michael and I, in rushing to finish, were avoiding the potential significance of ending. This perspective was valuable. I was able to see that Michael may have had some ambivalence about whether to continue or not, but was unable to contain conflicting feelings in a symbolic way. So I phoned Michael's house to say that a sixth session was still available.

Each ending is also a little death, and for Michael not lingering over the ending meant not dwelling on his father's death and the concomitant changes. But this avoidance was also mine; with hindsight I can see how I heaped the responsibility of decision-making upon Michael, as if I had no say at all in whether or not we should carry on. Another reason for shunning the full impact of conclusion is that, as David Edwards has it, 'the ending probes worth and value' (1997: 49). I had fears that nothing positive could be extracted from this encounter.

The final session

However, these reflections must have taken some time to crystallise, as the following week I had concerns that Michael would not be allowed to stand by his decision. Indeed, it transpired that he was going to come to the unit whatever he or I thought. Michael's community nurse and home manager, together with my supervisor, were of the opinion that we could go on with the sessions, that Michael had not had time to be able to make an informed choice about art therapy. I had a telephone conversation with the house manager, who reminded me of Michael's special interest in buses and proposed copying as an art activity, as Michael's 'autism' meant he 'had no imagination'. In retrospect, these points seem justified; many writers emphasise the length of time needed to form a working relationship with clients with autistic spectrum disorders (see, for example, Evans and Rutten-Saris, 1996), as well as pointing out the use of areas of personal interest to establish connections (for example, Bauer, 1996: 7).

At the time, though, I felt somewhat irritated. The discussion about Michael's treatment had taken place in my absence and, in a way, I had been given a taste of Michael's experience. The realities of power were different, but it still felt as if a degree of choice had been taken from me.

I began the sixth session with a sense of awkwardness, and doubts around whether a certain amount of 'coercion' was ethical or necessary in leading some individuals to therapy. In the event, such considerations seemed irrelevant. Somehow my strategic 'errors' had facilitated a shift in the therapeutic process, and in myself. Reluctance was still in the air; I asked Michael if he felt he had any say in whether or not to come, he replied, 'No'. But the wording of my question reflected a move towards greater openness. Early in the session Michael had also removed his coat; this involved a degree of bodily movement I would previously have found hard to imagine.

And, an unexpected new element had entered our work together. For Michael had brought to the art room a small photo album, which he clutched in one hand. The idea to bring this may well have originated with a member of the support staff at Michael's house; the mini-breakdown in therapy had a certain galvanising effect, bringing extra resources to bear on the encounter. But it was Michael's decision too; when I asked if he had chosen to bring the photographs along, he said 'Yes'. He also agreed that we could look at them together.

In this way imagery was introduced. Its presence at once opened up some 'potential space' and reduced the amount of 'no man's land' between us. Motion and a sense of aliveness began to creep back. I had to move nearer to Michael to look at the photos with him. We sat side by side, which seemed less confrontational than the just-off-facing position I had adopted in previous sessions.

We spent the bulk of the session painstakingly working our way through the album. Elements of paralysing anxiety remained; it was hard to judge the amount of time to spend on one picture, and I had to prompt Michael, when it seemed right, to flick over each plastic pocket. When I spoke, it felt impossible to put any body behind my words – an interesting echo of Michael's vocal quality. However, embryonic two-way communication had been established. There were snapshots of buses, housemates, a holiday. For what seemed like the first time, I heard Michael use words other than 'yes' or 'no' in describing the scenes: 'a hotel'; 'a boat'. Our increased physical proximity was not comfortable, but bearable. By the end of the session, we were about one-quarter of the way through the album.

Judy Weiser has noted how the 'realistic' nature of photographic imagery helps photos to function easily as transitional objects: 'Our mind achieves a cognitive leap that equates looking at the photo with being in the actual scene' (Weiser, 1993: 4). Photos can be a bridge between the concrete and symbolic. Lesley Fox adds that photographs are a useful way of exploring concepts of self, identity and bodily separateness, especially with autistic clients (Fox, 1998: 83–4). An album also highlights the role of the self in the context of the family or alternative social construct. Weiser (an art therapist) and others have defined 'PhotoTherapy' as a therapeutic approach in itself, emphasising the 'element of ordinariness to taking and discussing snapshots which is usually not evident in making or commenting on artistic creations' (Weiser, 1993: 11).

I fed back to Michael that he had brought a means of telling me more about himself to the session, even though he seemed to find being in the art room difficult. We could proceed one session at a time, Michael having the choice of ceasing attendance if he wanted.

The community nurse came to fetch Michael, and I smiled to myself as the former commented on the album, grabbed it and flicked through the pictures in two seconds flat.

Postscript

I now felt quite optimistic about the development of the therapeutic relationship, pondering ways of using Michael's special interest to engage him, and thinking that he might one day take his own photos during our sessions. So it was with a certain amount of dismay that I received a phone message the next week saying that Michael did not want to come to art therapy that day. This turned out to be more or less the last communication I had from him or his house.

Further information was gleaned from the Nurses' Outreach Team. Michael's mother had a confirmed date for her move out of the area. Michael seemed to be dealing with the news by withdrawing completely. He stopped coming to the Therapeutic Core Unit (to see me or the community nurse), instead taking to his bed and not eating properly. Christmas was near; such significant times can intensify the impact or memory of loss. It seemed clear that Michael, during our time together, had given me a strong taste of the way he is affected by bereavement and transition.

As part of the six-week assessment, I wrote to Michael and his house manager, saying that I understood he might be undergoing a difficult period in his life, but that the sessions were still open to him if he felt able to return.

After Christmas, there was some optimism that Michael might re-attend the unit. He had apparently enjoyed the festive season, going to a concert and a meal out with his housemates. The night before the session of 13 January would have taken place, I had a dream in which Michael – looking nothing like he does in reality – was an eager and skilful draughtsman, creating a drawing of a heavily armed and armoured tank, with an unerring eye for perspective and line. The bellicose nature of this image and its connotations of masculine power seemed at odds with Michael's timid presence. On the other hand, the tank perhaps spoke of his need for control, as well as conveying a metal plated defensiveness. The dream reminded me that I was a young male therapist, that there may have been an undercurrent of competitiveness between Michael and myself, and perhaps an unspoken element of anger. Hans Cohn discusses the etymological links between anger, anguish and anxiety; all are derived from the Latin 'angere', meaning 'to squeeze, to strangle'. Thus, 'restriction, tightness and strangulation are the physical aspects of an emotional state' (Cohn, 1997: 69).

When I wrote my original case study, art therapy sessions remained nominally open for Michael though he showed little sign of returning. Perhaps the lack of resolution around ending resonated with any unresolved feelings Michael may have had in connection with his father's death. For my part, writing represented an important move towards closure.

Conclusion

In the face of a therapeutic encounter where there is a baffling response or lack of response, the process of writing can contribute to a symbolic redemption of experiential confusion. Writing can also involve a certain 'encapsulation'; perhaps a parallel to one type of reaction to bewilderment characteristic of the autistic continuum.

In this chapter, I have considered how Michael's behaviour might have been informed by both neurophysiological and psychodynamic factors. These are probably intertwined, or at least extremely hard to separate in reality. In the final analysis, it is our experience of such clients that is important; how much we are able to feel in their presence, finding an approach conducive to empathy. The latter is often hard to achieve in relation to people with autistic features.

My time with Michael was also characterised by a lack of image-making activity – a kind of creative block – which made me think about possible ways forward for art therapy in working with this client group. If there was 'no-man's land' between Michael and myself, there also seemed to be some distance between the various professional approaches to AS. Art therapy, often not a highly valued treatment intervention in this context, might be able to adapt and incorporate the kind of directive strategies used by psychologists/educationalists, while at the same time having a lot to offer on its own terms, in the development of symbolisation and tolerance to more open-ended goals. A tendency towards predominantly visual thinking in those with Asperger's Syndrome would also point to the potential effectiveness of art therapy.

The work with Michael did not have the chance to progress beyond the very early stages of learning to understand and be with each other. Michael's initial resistance to communication – visual or verbal – began to give way, in the sixth session, to a desire to reveal something of himself to me. In the event, there may have been too much change in his life for him to continue to attend art therapy. Yet some movement had begun to enter both our spheres of competence and control: Michael's constricted psychic space, my expectations of cure, creativity or visible betterment for my clients.

Afterword

If I were a time-travelling supervisor, the salient piece of advice I would give is: don't worry about the lack of art making. It's by no means the norm for clients (especially in this area) to engage fearlessly with the materials and spew out fascinating pictures. The images are there anyway, in your reflections and descriptions; and eventually they might emerge (as here) concretely, unexpectedly.

On the other hand, I'm less afraid in my current practice of making art work myself. Some people seem to need this, to give flesh to their feelings or narrative; perhaps as a child might exhort the parent to 'draw a boat! Draw an alien!' Bragge and Fenner's account of the 'Interactive Square' (2009) really resonates with me, especially in their article's challenge to the idea that visual art is the preserve of the solo romantic in his garret. Art making now is simply the main interactive/ expressive tool in my armoury. I also routinely use sound, speech, playful enactment, movement and even physical contact in my sessions with people with learning disabilities (including clients on the autistic spectrum).

But would I approach this particular encounter any differently with the benefit of hind (or fore) sight? Perhaps. I might, for example, present information about the therapy in a different way: in written form, or augmented by photos and pictures (some autistic clients use 'Social Stories' – descriptions of an event or idea in terms of appropriate social responses – to help orient them in various interpersonal situations). I would be more alert to small, practical variations such as changing my seating position (the side-by-side arrangement is a mainstay of mentalisation-based approaches, in which the focus is continually directed towards conceptualising the thoughts of the other). I could have made earlier contact with Michael's support staff, professionals (often undervalued) who spend lots of time with service users and are an important resource. And I may have kept the aim of assessment more to the front of my mind.

Would oiling the cogs of the process in this way dilute the raw affective dynamics of the encounter? It is hard to know; the transference–countertransference complex is a play of fluid intersubjectivity (and here I find Stern's conceptions helpful) rather than an unchanging monolithic entity. My responses as a seasoned practitioner would differ from those of a novice, and Michael's reactions would then (perhaps) change in their turn. One thing I do envy my trainee self is an acute sensitivity to detail, which tends to fade with experience.

Two related, unchanging factors would be, I believe, the enabling support of the institution and the central importance of clinical supervision. The latter is a core principle of psychodynamic psychotherapy worth preserving as practice shifts in an era of evidence-based practice and commissioning.

It was helpful to consult literature from the psychology field when this study was first composed. There seemed a dearth of writing about the use of art therapy with autistic adults, particularly those at the 'high functioning' end of the spectrum. This lack has since been remedied to an extent: see, for example, Robin Tipple's 2007 paper on brief art therapy work with a young person with Asperger's Syndrome.

A final note on Michael himself. I know that he was able to return to art therapy, attending individual sessions with my supervisor from the placement described here; these lasted for a year or so. Once again he spoke little, but did make art work; geometrical drawings perhaps not that far removed from my intuition in dream (though less bellicose!). My hope is that Michael's initial experience resonated on some level. He was at least resilient enough to use a further opportunity for art therapy input when it presented itself.

References

American Psychiatric Association (1994) *Diagnostic and Statistical Manual of Mental Disorders (DSM-IV)*, 4th edition, Washington, DC: American Psychiatric Association.

Attwood, T. (1998) *Asperger's Syndrome: A Guide for Parents and Professionals*, London: Elizabeth Kingsley.

Bauer, S. (1996) *Asperger Syndrome: Through the Lifespan.* Website of the Developmental Unit, The Genesee Hospital, New York. Online. Available at: www.aspennj.org/pdf/information/articles/aspergers-syndrome-through-the-lifespan.pdf (accessed May 2000).

Bragge, A. and Fenner, P. (2009) 'The emergence of the "Interactive Square" as an approach to art therapy with children on the autistic spectrum', *International Journal of Art Therapy: Inscape*, 14 (1): 17–28.

Cohn, H. (1997) *Existential Thought and Therapeutic Practice*, London: Sage.
Cundall, A.M. (1991) 'Resistance', MA Thesis, University of Hertfordshire School of Art and Design.
Edwards, D. (1997) 'Endings', *Inscape*, 2 (2): 49–53.
Evans, K. (1998) 'Shaping experience and sharing meaning: art therapy for children with autism', *Inscape*, 3 (1): 25–41.
Evans, K. and Rutten-Saris, M. (1996) 'Shaping vitality affects: enriching communication art therapy for children with autism'. Transcript of lecture given at Leeds Conference, *The Uses and Applications of Art Therapy*.
Fox, L. (1998) 'Lost in space: the relevance of art therapy with clients who have autism or autistic features' in Rees, M. (ed.), *Drawing on Difference: Art Therapy with People with Learning Disabilities*, London: Routledge, pp. 74–89.
Klin, A. and Volkmar, F. (1995) *Asperger Syndrome: Guidelines for Treatment and Intervention*, PDD Website: Learning Disabilities Association of America. Online. Available at: www.margaretkay.com/uploads/asdiagnosis.pdf (accessed May 2000).
Newham, P. (1998) *Therapeutic Voicework*, London: Elizabeth Kingsley.
Stack, M. (1998) 'Humpty Dumpty's shell: working with autistic defence mechanisms' in Rees, M. (ed.), *Drawing on Difference: Art Therapy with People with Learning Disabilities*, London: Routledge, pp. 91–119.
Tantam, D. (1992) *Asperger Syndrome*, Birmingham: University of Birmingham School of Education.
Tipple, R. (2007) 'Paranoia and paracosms: brief art therapy with a youngster with Asperger's Syndrome' in Case, C. and Dalley, T. (eds), *Art Therapy with Children: From Infancy to Adolescence*, London: Routledge, pp. 175–92.
Weiser, J. (1993) *PhotoTherapy*, San Francisco: Jossey-Bass.
Wing, L. (1981) 'Asperger's Syndrome: a clinical account', *Psychological Medicine*, 11: 115–29.

Chapter 3

Emptiness and silence

Art therapy with a child with autism

Sue Ginsberg

>Shut up. Shut up. There's nobody here.
>If you think you hear somebody knocking on the other side of the words, pay
>No attention. It will be only
>The great creature that thumps its tail
>On silence on the other side.
>If you do not even hear that
>I'll give the beast a quick skelp
>And through art you'll hear it yelp...
>
>W.S. Graham, 'The Beast in the Space'

Introduction

This chapter discusses the core features of emptiness and silence in the art therapy process with a boy with autism who had very little language, whom I will call Peter. His art therapy sessions took place in the context of his special school.

Emptiness and silence do not always go together. A pause can be 'pregnant', and words can be empty. In art therapy sessions with Peter, silence was related to his lack of words and to the way that my own words seemed empty when I was with him. The space between us was not just to do with the absence of words but the sense that I was searching for him over some unfathomable distance of separation. In fact, much of what happened in sessions with Peter initially was to do with being with him, and my seeking him out in the space between us. This sometimes felt like a chasm, and at other times seemed denied and non-existent.

Art therapy is not dependent on words and art therapists have different views as to how they are used in sessions, but words, along with the art making, give form to experience. As sessions progressed, Peter was more able to receive, digest and respond to my words and also became more communicative himself. However, he constantly struggled with feelings that threatened to become overwhelming, and his need for containment and regulation became prominent themes in sessions. His use of art materials acted as a bridge between us, although it could also become a wall to keep me out.

Autism is a communication disorder and it affects the way thinking and communicating happen in schools and families. It is particularly challenging to find a way of sharing insights about someone who has little or no language, because words have to be used to describe feeling states and experiences that are pre-verbal and which have not been previously articulated. It was important to find ways of thinking about him with those who lived and worked with him, and I was aware that the struggle to make sense of what was happening could reinforce feelings of emptiness and 'not knowing' in everyone.

Working with Peter required an approach that could keep thinking alive for both of us in the sessions, and also for parents and staff. We could all find ourselves unable to think, anxious about keeping the environment manageable for him, and enormously frustrated in the struggle to try and make sense of his experience. There was a danger of colluding with his desperate demands for a totally predictable world with omniscient people around him who could know exactly what he needed at all times and who could provide for his every need. The key for me was being alert to what was happening in the countertransference, and my reverie, as I gave time to him. I found Stern's (1985) ideas about how mothers attune to their babies' feeling states helpful here, especially as I attempted to tune in to his experience with the art materials.

The desire to fill the void, or to avoid the feeling of emptiness, was present not only for Peter, but also for me. His use of materials and my use of words could become compensatory, which would then limit or even close up the potential opportunity for growth and development. Knowing when and how to intervene so that a different thought might be risked without falling into the void was a challenge. However, his engagement with art materials gave expression to his internal state; form could be given to feelings in the space between us, and along with an emerging sense of self there could be moments of full, shared experience and understanding.

I will consider the process of art therapy with Peter, including looking at two sessions, one from the early part of the work with him and another later on. The themes of emptiness and silence will be explored, and the associated need to experience regulation and containment in managing his feelings. As the therapy progressed, the felt space between us changed; there were gradual developments in his art work, and through his drawings in particular he created a safe place for himself to be seen and to occupy.

The work in context

Working in schools places its own demands on art therapy. Sessions can only be offered during term time, there are timetabling constraints, difficulties in finding times to liaise with teaching staff, as well as a whole host of other issues in the way art therapy and the art therapist are perceived and how this work can happen alongside everything else that is high on the agenda within an educational setting. Schools are concerned with target setting and are task orientated, and art therapy is a process that is difficult to measure. Art therapy supports emotional and cognitive development and it could be seen as sharing the same overall aim of schools which is to facilitate learning (Dalley, 1990; Karkou 1999).

The work discussed here was in a special educational setting: a primary school for pupils with moderate learning difficulties (MLD). Peter took up a place in the resource base for pupils with autism, which was part of the school and aimed to help children integrate into other school activities and classes as appropriate.

In order to work effectively as an art therapist in a special school, it is important that there should be regular and thoughtful communication with staff and parents. This can be difficult to achieve, particularly with teachers, as there are already many demands on their time. It is very valuable, however, if the benefit of thinking about a pupil's emotional needs and how they relate to the external world, is recognised. When working with children with autism, the communication difficulty that is already present can also make it difficult for people around them to think and communicate effectively. For instance, the emptiness and silence in the sessions with Peter seemed to be present outside the art therapy room. It was difficult for me to find the words. How can pre-verbal feeling states be talked about? Is it possible for people who are often tired and stressed to bear looking at the fears that cannot be faced by the child? Just as any space for thought can be anticipated by the individual with autism as being an empty black hole (Tustin, 1990: 91), so those who work with that person may themselves unconsciously avoid engaging with clear thinking. Finding opportunities to think together about how to help the child to know that fears can be recognised, withstood and held, is a vital part of the work of the art therapist.

The fear of change for a child with autism can very easily become the parents' fear (Klauber, 1999: 33), and this can also apply to those who work with the child, including the art therapist. It is easy to become stuck in ways of doing things, without challenging the child's rigid routines, for fear of the terrible disruption it may cause.

I changed my timetable at the beginning of the autumn term after the summer break, which meant that Peter's art therapy session was moved to a time that was half an hour later. Waiting in his classroom became intolerable for him and he could not manage his anxiety even though changes to activities were set out as visual timetables and carefully talked about. Within two weeks there were pleas from his teachers to revert to the old time. I felt that it would be helpful if the storm could be weathered in order for him to accept the change. After a number of positive discussions with staff in which I had a real sense of how difficult it was to contain him at this time within the group, we reached a compromise of having the session a quarter of an hour earlier. This continued to be difficult for him and everyone around him, but he eventually managed the change. I was aware of the anxiety Peter carried with him which was directly associated with his fear of gaps: the frantic need to know that he was not 'dropped'. Pecotic describes a patient's similar distressed response to waiting as seeming 'to reflect some elemental terror rising out of the fear of being forgotten and abandoned by me as a person who kept him in mind'(1999: 147). Peter's dread of this gap in waiting had become the dread of everyone in the classroom. However, as time went on, real effort was given to helping him to know that he could not impose his omnipotent demands on everyone, and that the adults around him could work together to show that both he and they could survive the consequences.

One of the main features shaping any work in schools is the rhythm of the school year. There are regular breaks, which have to be planned for carefully and which powerfully affect the art therapy process. Coping with these breaks and returning to school after a weekend or a holiday was difficult. Peter did not seem to be able to make sense of visual charts in art therapy in order to prepare for a break except when we were working towards the actual end of the therapy itself. Of course, learning over time that these frequent gaps were not catastrophic provided him with rehearsals of the real ending. He appeared to be able to use our survival of breaks in art therapy to make developmental gains. It was as if he was confronted with a thought that was focused and real, and although related to the anxiety around change (and perhaps with this the feeling that he could fall into nothingness), this thought also alluded to a break in relationship, which in itself acknowledged that some form of relating existed. Case (2000) explores the impact of breaks on therapy and describes how the development of thought can be prompted by absence; it allows something to be thought of, and the ensuing frustration can then lead to cognitive development.

Peter

Peter was five when he was referred to art therapy, and I worked with him for nearly three years. He lived with his mother, father and older brother in a stable, caring family, and his autism had been evident from an early age. He sometimes gesticulated in an idiosyncratic way, and generally made few attempts to communicate his needs. His teacher felt that art therapy would contribute to the school's assessment and understanding of him.

Peter struggled to access learning in his school setting. He rarely tolerated being in a group and quickly established obsessions and autistic routines. It was impossible to know 'where he was'. To those who worked with him, it felt as if there was another Peter waiting to emerge or to be found, but who was hidden from sight behind the wall of his autism. Sometimes he could surprise people with a simple, straightforward response. This gave a glimpse or promise of someone able to relate in an ordinary way, but usually he seemed out of reach and enigmatic. He was generally stuck within his own systems, strategies and obsessions, through which he attempted to make sense of, or to manage, his experience. These systems and strategies often failed him as they relied on cues that could not incorporate the unpredictable nature of human behaviour and events. When this happened, it was as if the ground disappeared under his feet. A teaching assistant came to school one day in the tracksuit she would only normally wear when it was 'swimming day'. He understood this as a communication that he would be going on the bus to the swimming pool, and nothing would convince him otherwise. The upset and anger arising from this confusion was so difficult to contain in the classroom that the member of staff concerned even considered going home to change her clothes. Initially of course, it was unclear as to why Peter was so upset, and only gradually did it become apparent. Much of the concern of the staff working with him was about how to contain his ensuing rages on these occasions. A 'time out' room was allocated for him to go into (with two adults) when his safety or the safety of other people and property was at risk.

Early sessions

I offered Peter a few basic art materials with the addition of water in a water tray, and a cornflour and water mixture. I provided these to give an opportunity for sensory exploration, which I felt might match his level of development. The cornflour mixture was what primarily absorbed and preoccupied him, and he immersed himself in it until there was nothing left. Each week he returned to the cornflour, initially slurping it straight from the tray, or using his hands to 'feed' himself, and at the same time keeping me out as he was fully intent only on taking this in. At times he wanted to actually sit in it, or to climb into the water tray. Sometimes he would sit on the table to eat, after sweeping everything else onto the floor, and once he sat on my lap with the tray in front of him. I felt very maternal towards him, as if I were holding a nursing baby. It seemed that for him any gaps were intolerable. He could not allow an opening for me as a different object or for anything else in the room; at any rate certainly not until he had experienced some form of infilling. When I thought about the potential space between us, I experienced either no space, or a void that extinguished my words in flight like the popping of empty, aimless bubbles. The reflective space of the sessions was sucked dry, airless and closed up along with any opportunity for him to allow a sense of 'not me'.

As sessions progressed in the first few months, I wanted to find ways of attuning to him, and to open up an awareness of there being two people in the room. His desire to 'absorb' could be represented in different forms using art materials, and over the next few months this absorbing was one of the main themes of the sessions. At this time, it was helpful to consider Evans' and Rutten-Saris' use of Stern's concept of 'vitality affects' (the undefined and unseparated elements of early sensory and emotional experience) in their work with children with autism (1998: 57). I experienced 'baby' Peter through his soaking, sucking, absorbing, and then emptying, spitting out, and spilling.

The cornflour mixture was dripped onto paper, and as it was soaked up he then scraped off and ate the drying pieces. His scratch marks were there to be seen on the paper (Figure 3.1), and gave lasting form to this experience. Later on, he tore pieces off to suck dry and spit out, and as this developed he used me as the place where the sucked pieces would be discarded (first in my hand and then in a pot). When he had used up the cornflour, he drenched sheets of paper in the water tray,

Figure 3.1 Scratch marks in cornflour and water

sometimes stuffing these in his mouth to suck or just dropping them dripping to the floor. He wanted to do this over and over again. Peter became preoccupied with these activities: soaking up or being filled, and spilling out or tipping over. He tested my ability to provide containment every week by regularly trying to spill the water or the paints. Sometimes he was so quick that he tipped out the water from the tray all over the floor, squealing excitedly. Once, early on, he urinated in the water tray. I was too late to prevent this but quickly emptied it and flushed out the tray with clean water as he watched. I sensed that he found this tipping out quite exciting and I was concerned that more acceptable ways of working with these themes could be found. On subsequent weeks the desire to empty and spill out could be explored more appropriately by using the taps to fill a smaller tray with water which we could then tip out together, with a growing awareness of regulating and containing the flow. He often put his finger up to the spout on the tap as the water flowed out; not, it seemed, to see it spurt out under pressure, but to feel the hole and the fullness of the flow as it pushed against his finger.

The preoccupation with eating the cornflour mixture continued over some months. He always went to this first and remained fixated until there was none left. Afterwards he would then engage in spilling and tipping, and this became the pattern of the sessions. Filling and emptying. There was no space allowed for reflection or development. Words could not be received. It seemed as though what initially had delighted and satisfied him had become an automatic, obsessive and mechanistic response to the materials. I began to think about slowly reducing the amount of cornflour liquid, which for him had become so addictive. I wondered what his response would be to this. Would he think that I was a cruel mother who was taking away what he needed to fill himself with and feel safe? How could I do this when he felt so empty and would be left with nothing? I felt guilty that I would not be continuing to provide something which he at times seemed so desperate for. I also thought about his demand for perfection in others in order that he could be sure that they could meet his needs, and the violent consequences when he was left with a gap that could not be filled.

The following account describes parts of the twenty-third session when for the first time, after a gradual reduction, there was no provision of cornflour liquid. Peter immediately noticed the absence. He searched, looking for the tray and trying to open cupboards. He had never looked for anything before, and I acknowledged the search. He vocalised his annoyance, but did not persist. Much of what happened in the next ten minutes or so was familiar and frenetic: filling and tipping out water at the sink, soaking paper in water then dropping it onto the floor, attempting to tip up the water tray (which I prevented), spitting into the water, stuffing paper into his mouth and running with it, seemingly wanting me to take it out. He then took some modelling material and put lumps in the water which he chewed and spat out onto the floor. I again provided a pot to hold the pieces as an instinctive response to offer some containment, which he used. Suddenly he bolted out of the door and ran down the corridor before I could stop him. However, at the end, he was waiting for me to reach him, and there was a feeling of delight in being retrieved. Back in the room, I said 'Peter needs Sue to keep hold of him and all the pieces'. He was looking at me and listening, and put his arms around me, in what seemed to be a direct response to the word 'hold'. I was surprised and moved by this. There seemed to be some recognition that I could be trusted to do the holding for him when he needed it. Shortly afterwards, he would have urinated in the water tray again, but I managed to lead him to the toilet which he used, returning calmly to continue the session.

Discussion

My impression of Peter over these first six months was of a hungry baby who needed to be filled up, and who wanted only mother's milk; not her feelings or her mind. As he slurped his way through the liquid cornflour, cutting himself off from me, all that could be experienced was physical infilling. This absorbing sensory activity protected him from the threat of impingement and the void he felt he might fall into. Bick's (1968) notion of a 'second skin' was a helpful aid to understanding this way of protecting himself from catastrophic anxieties in order to hold things together. It seemed to me that there was a dread of interior and exterior spaces, which meant that they had to be closed and 'filled' or he would be lost completely. His feeding ritual meant that what he was taking in left no room for anything else, and to some extent this was true of other routines that he developed later on. Alvarez (1999: 72) describes autistic rituals as being set up to fulfil, in part, normal psychological needs. They are to do with taking something in, as well as keeping things out. If one is removed, another is quickly established in its place, in order to fill the gap. For Peter, of course, his liquid 'feed' was not ever-flowing and so he could not continue ad infinitum. When it was used up, he was unable to hold things in; they spilled out and overflowed. The 'fear of being spilled and of flowing away into nothingness' (Tustin, 1996: 49) was present, and he struggled to contain his feelings. Art materials provide many opportunities for spilling, but there is also the possibility of containment through the therapist's response. For Peter, the process of absorbing and eating could be seen and preserved in marks on paper. Sucked pieces of paper and modelling material could be held together in a container. There was then tangible evidence of 'something' being brought together, rather than a spilling out or dropping into 'nothingness'. His own bodily spillages, in the form of urine, could also begin to be contained, and shortly after this session he learned how to sign 'toilet' and regulate this for himself.

The way he used the art materials carried with it indications of feelings and states of mind that could not be expressed with words. He cut himself off from me and, as described earlier, my own words seemed to disappear into a void or were shut out. His communications to me were non-verbal and I had the impression that they were like the side effects of his spilled out feelings. This may be because children with autism do not project feelings in the ordinary way (Reid, 1999); however, I often felt the anxiety in the room and my own feelings were of central importance in guiding what I was consciously reflecting back to him. These included my response to his sensory experience with the art materials. Overall, he engendered in me the feelings of a maternal object who needed to hold him together, and to keep in mind what was good for him.

Initially, I used very few words when I was with Peter, but I was aware that gradually over time I had a greater sense of him listening, and the space between us became more dynamic. I wondered whether his returning experience of me after the break was of a mother who had dropped the baby in him. He responded to the word 'hold' and, with it, communicated something about his own capacity to hold onto me and my thoughts about him. This was the first time in art therapy he had searched for anything, and he had also created a different space between us – one which, in running away, he had also waited for me and held me in mind. It seemed that the emptiness he was confronted with through the loss of the cornflour and the previous week's break had prompted a development in thinking and relating.

The empty space of the paper

Three weeks later, Peter moved on to more solid forms of expression. He began to use different art materials, showing a particular preference for felt pens. This once more became ritualised, and I often felt that this process was perpetuated by a sort of anxiety-driven conveyor belt; even if he had thought of stopping, there was a feeling that he did not know how to, and that he also could not conceive that there could be something else to take its place. However, there were developments in his drawings which, although slow and sometimes almost imperceptible, were nonetheless real.

Peter began to make face schemas. Initially it was as if he could not allow them to be left exposed. He obliterated them, sometimes filling the paper with an anxious energy of dense scribble that blocked out any form; a spilling out of line reminiscent of the liquid feeling states (Figure 3.2). As the therapy progressed, the faces were given space to be seen and to remain (Figure 3.3). These drawings probably held no symbolic or representational meaning for Peter, but they seemed to be a place where, at a pre-verbal level, expressions of internal states could be held. As I looked back over his work, it provided me with something like a time map of these states. I was struck by the closing of the space in his images in the session after an unplanned break (I had missed a session because of a bereavement). Although I had noticed the change and had talked to him about not being there as he expected me to be, it was only later that I made the connection between the 'squashed', almost unrecognisable faces that he had produced (Figure 3.4), and my sudden disappearance which was due to a death. At the time, loss and a felt absence was very much my experience. I was perhaps aware that for both of us, it was painful. Something had closed up; the gap could not be looked at. He was fretful about other gaps around this time: for instance, he hated it if I left some buttons on my cardigan unfastened, as if he thought I needed to be held together. I began to make marks alongside him, because this seemed to be the only way to be with him and to keep alive the fact that another person was curious about him.

Figure 3.2 Felt pens

44 Sue Ginsberg

Figure 3.3 Faces

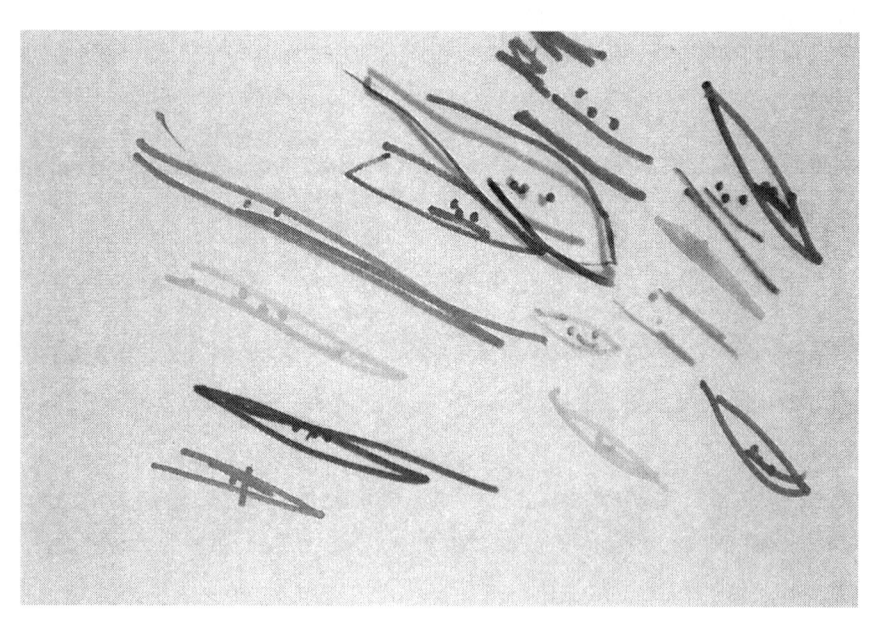

Figure 3.4 Squashed faces

He allowed me to do this, and sometimes joined in with me. He also accepted my support in regulating the number of pen pots and sheets of paper he used. There was a sense of an emerging self, which was gradually allowed exposure in his schematic face drawings.

Later on: a sense of balance

The following session took place two years into his art therapy. Peter continued to struggle with being part of a group in his classroom, and often chose to go into his 'time out' room when he felt he could not contain his feelings. On this particular day he had not arrived for his session, and after a few minutes I went to his classroom to find out what had happened. He was in the 'time out' room with two adults. I was told that there was something about his plimsolls that he was upset about, but it was unclear what the problem was. I greeted him and said it was time for art therapy. He took his plimsolls to put them on in order to come with me, but he could not find a way of doing this. They were fastened with Velcro and he had difficulty organising his thoughts to first undo them so that they could go on his feet. He refused help and vocalised fretfully. I wondered about the emotional connotations of 'undoing' but wanting to put things together. Eventually, unsettled, he came to art therapy with me without his shoes. A teaching assistant waited outside the room in case support was needed. In the room, he immediately swept all the art materials off the table (except the paint, which I rescued), and banged his head and hands repeatedly against the filing cabinet. I said, 'Peter is so upset ... he can't think', and that I was thinking about him and his feelings. There were pens, pencils, crayons and pots all over the floor, and he was running around the room. I suggested he use the large mat to keep safe because it was clear of objects. This seemed to resonate with the safe space of 'time out', and he readily used it. He gradually calmed down, and lay on the mat with his feet in the air. After a while, he got up and began a pattern of jumping little jumps, then rolling down to the mat again. He stood on one leg touching the wall for support and rolled down. He got up and repeated the same sequence several times. I felt that this was a powerful image of how he was feeling, and acknowledged the fact that he was standing on one leg, not two, and perhaps he could fall, but he felt in control. He had a leg to balance on.

Peter came and sat at the table to draw. I picked up the things on the floor and then sat with him. He drew a variety of marks, but mainly faces, wanting to use up all the paper. As I sat with him and also used art materials, he twice gave me a pen to draw with, which he had rarely done before. A few minutes before the end of the session, I reminded him that there would be no more pen pots (regulating the number of times he could go through all the pens in turn before beginning again with another pot was necessary in preparing to finish). He protested loudly in response to this, but afterwards moved to the mat and stood on one leg again. I said that even though it felt as if he was on the edge, he could manage on one leg with support. He went over to the whiteboard and briefly used the pens there to cover a crack on the board with little marks. It was then time to stop and he left the room, composed, to return to his class.

Discussion

Art therapy is a 'come as you are' time. Sometimes in schools, I am asked about whether a pupil has 'been good', or children are asked if they've 'had fun'. In this context, it is important that the child knows what the art therapist's expectations are. Peter was able to respond to my invitation to him to come as he was, with or without shoes; able or not able to hold things together. On this occasion there seemed to be the recognition that the space in the art therapy room was a place he could occupy even though he was upset. This session had a different quality to it from those earlier on when Peter would either fill up (and in so doing avoid the emptiness of the time), or deny the space between us. The potential space therefore seemed more accessible. The potential space, in Winnicott's terms, is a place where play happens (Winnicott, 1971: 47). Play leads to development, relationships, and communication. Can this be available to children with autism who, at the extreme end of the spectrum, 'with the "potential space" unavailable or shut down', are 'fixed in the here and now, without access to memory or anticipation and living in fear of attack by unmodified instinctual feelings'(Fox, 1998: 76)? Is this space always shut down? Although Peter's activity in the room would not be described as conventional early play, he engaged in a process of enactment that conveyed a similar task of representation. It seemed to me that Peter had been able to achieve something for himself that was not ruled by his autism. What had allowed him to access this? It could be that he again recognised the emotional holding that was offered. The room became a physical container for his uncontained feelings, and there appeared to be no fear of emptiness in the space between us. Even in his upset, Peter was able to hear and respond to my suggestion that the mat could be a containing place for him. It provided him with a space with edges, as opposed to his feeling of being 'on the edge', a precarious position to be in. Internal processes were being enacted through his use of the objects, boundaries and space of the room. There was a sense that through my thinking about his emotional experience, he was able to find his own place for thought, and therefore the therapeutic relationship, not just the physical space of the room, was a key factor. This relates to Bion's (1962) concept of the maternal object as container for the infant's primitive feelings, enabling the subsequent development of a capacity for thought.

Although Peter approached the art materials in much the same way as always, there was a new element between us: an awareness of a shared space. Figure 3.5 shows his drawing of a face that seems to be teetering on a mark that could be seen to be a sort of leg. On the other hand, the eyes and nose have space within them, and there is a balloon-like, blown-up quality about the image. The mark at the bottom could almost be anchoring the head to keep it from floating away. There is the prototype of something to prevent it (albeit rather tentatively) either from falling down or from drifting off up into space.

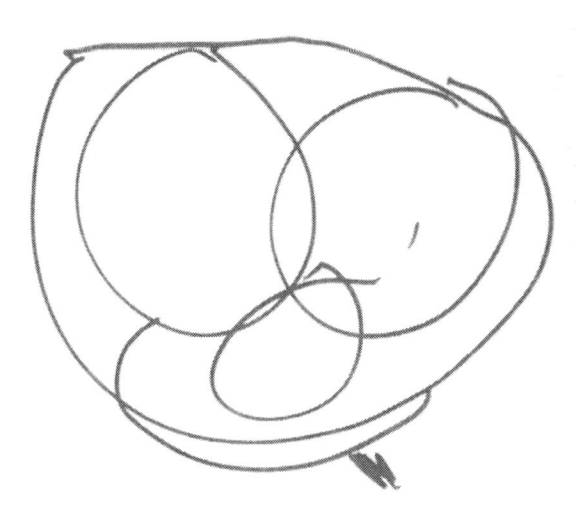

Figure 3.5 Teetering

These reflections are mine, and not Peter's, but perhaps there were moments when the 'unmodified instinctual feelings' referred to earlier could be held and processed, so that images as well as thoughts could emerge.

Drawing to a close

Soon after this, Peter was offered a place in a specialist school for children with autism, and as a consequence we had to think about ending art therapy. A new, manic element entered these last sessions. He would rush excitedly around the room, looking at me and giggling as if to draw me into a sort of dance to keep up with him. He threw art materials onto the floor, turned lights off and on, and tried to bolt out of the room. Each week, he would move the empty water tray along, and then curl up in it to press his body against the hard sides. When he precipitously stood up in it to jump out, I was concerned that in this mindless state he would fall, and drew closer to support him. He flopped heavily onto me to be lifted down. These routines happened each week until the last session, when he was calm and contained, but unwilling to listen to me talking about 'goodbye', and would not fill in the remaining space on the chart counting down the sessions. He rushed his drawings, using many sheets of paper, but his 'faces' were there to be seen (Figure 3.6).

I felt there was not enough time and wondered if Peter felt this too. He rushed around, testing the physical and therapeutic boundaries of the sessions, and drawing me into thinking about him. In contrast to earlier on, he was actively seeking me out, needing support to manage his move. In his last session, he recognised the boundary of the finishing line. It was clear and certain, although he

Figure 3.6 Peter's last session

appeared to avoid thinking about it. As he left, he signed 'lunch', and I felt that he was able to move on to what there was for him outside the room, without me.

Conclusion

In art therapy, Peter moved from a state of fluidity towards an awareness of containment, where the threat of emptiness and formlessness could be shared and survived. Through the experience of being held in mind, he began to develop a sense of his own edges, and to find a place for himself. This meant that he could gradually begin to regulate feelings and express certain needs. He became more communicative, and the feeling of emptiness, silence or dead space between us changed as he risked interaction.

The use of art materials and the physical space in the room became the arena in which this could take place. His repetitive drawing could be a space for hiding as well as revealing; for locking me out, or for drawing me in.

Afterword

There is often a quiet, concentrated separateness in the absorbing act of making art. This can easily become a means of retreat for children with autism. If they do choose to use art materials, it can become a way of avoiding relating to another person. At the heart of effective therapy is relationship, so in art therapy there is the question of how this space can become shared. Anne Alvarez talks about 'finding the wavelength' in therapy with children with autism (2008); the need to be robust and active in seeking out signs of relatedness, and actually employing the very areas of autistic impairment: symbolic capacity, social interaction and play. Although she is not referring to art therapy, this is very relevant to the work that I do with children. Art therapy addresses all these areas of deficit; it takes place within a relationship that offers the hope and expectation that communication, attachment, and play can happen. When I attempted to draw alongside Peter in sessions, my marks together with my words were often ignored. I have noticed subsequently that shared attention using art materials can begin within a sort of rhythm, a kinetic playfulness.

If this work with Peter were to start now, would it be the same as it was then? Now, I am less hesitant about using materials actively alongside children with autism. At a basic physical level of experience, this provides the potential to be seen and heard when there are few words. There is a sense that I can be a more active partner; I may be more directive in navigating the space of the session, in 'seeking out signs of relatedness', without feeling that in some way I am undermining the psychodynamic process. However, I have to be constantly alert to what is drawing me into any particular 'way' of relating. Is a child's need for structure – and therefore my desire to provide a negotiable environment – governing the sense that a 'plan' is needed? Is my helplessness at being ignored and excluded enticing me into wanting to take control? Is waiting in silence a place that I need to inhabit with a child, even if that feels empty and lifeless? Opening up a potential space with Peter was the main focus of his art therapy and would still be if we were to start this work today. I would still need to be present to emptiness and silence. I would still need to wait for him. However, the use of art materials provides a way for the therapist to notice, show interest, be curious, 'find the wavelength' and to help give physical form and thought to primitive communications.

References

Alvarez, A. (1999) 'Disorder, deviance and personality: factors in the persistence and modifiability of autism' in Alvarez, A. and Reid, S. (eds), *Autism and Personality*, London: Routledge.
—— (2008) 'Finding the wavelength: tools in communication with children with autism', in Barrows, K. (ed.), *Autism in Childhood and Autistic Features in Adults A Psychoanalytic Perspective* [e-book], London: Karnac. Available through Anglia Ruskin University Library website at: http://libweb.anglia.ac.uk (accessed 12 July 2012).
Bick, E. (1968) 'The experience of the skin in early object relations', *International Journal of Psycho-Analysis*, 49: 484–6.
Bion, W.R. (1962) *Learning from Experience*, London: Karnac.
Case, C. (2000) 'Santa's grotto: an exploration of the Christmas break in therapy', *Inscape*, 5 (1): 11–18.
Dalley, T. (1990) 'Images and integration: art therapy in a multi-cultural school' in Case, C. and Dalley, T. (eds), *Working with Children in Art Therapy*, London: Routledge.

Evans, K. and Rutten-Saris, M. (1998) 'Shaping vitality affects, enriching communication: art therapy for children with autism' in Sandle, D. (ed.), *Development and Diversity: New Applications in Art Therapy*, London and New York: Free Association Books.

Fox, L. (1998) 'Lost in space: the relevance of art therapy with clients who have autism or autistic features', in Rees, M. (ed.), *Drawing on Difference: Art Therapy with People Who Have Learning Difficulties*, London and New York: Routledge.

Graham, W.S. (1996) 'The Beast in the Space', *The Oxford Anthology of Great English Poetry II: Blake to Heaney*, Oxford: Oxford University Press.

Karkou, V. (1999) 'Art therapy in education: findings from a nationwide survey in arts therapies', *Inscape*, 4 (2): 62–9.

Klauber, T. (1999) 'The significance of trauma and other factors in work with the parents of children with autism' in Alvarez, A. and Reid, S. (eds), *Autism and Personality*, London: Routledge.

Pecotic, B. (1999) 'Edward: lost and found: from passive withdrawal to symbolic functioning' in Alvarez, A. and Reid, S. (eds), *Autism and Personality*, London: Routledge.

Reid, S. (1999) 'The assessment of the child with autism: a family perspective' in Alvarez, A. and Reid, S. (eds), *Autism and Personality*, London: Routledge.

Stern, D. (1985) *The Interpersonal World of the Infant*, New York: Basic Books.

Tustin, F. (1990) *The Protective Shell in Children and Adults*, London and New York: Karnac Books.

——(1996) 'The emergence of a sense of Self, or the development of "I-ness"' in Richards, V. (ed.), *The Person who is Me: Contemporary Perspectives on the True and False Self*, London: Karnac Books.

Winnicott, D.W. (1971) *Playing and Reality*, London: Tavistock.

Chapter 4

A group of five autistic young adults

Penelope Wilson

Introduction

This study looks at an art therapy group of five autistic young adults. The members were near in age and they used the art materials creatively to negotiate very early stages of development. All except one of the clients knew each other well, as they lived together in the same group home. Thus they were at ease within the group and familiar with the routine, whereas a group of such clients usually takes many weeks to establish a sense of safety from which to begin exploring for themselves.

The group had been meeting for six months before I joined them as part of my art therapy training. My supervisor clearly managed the group on her own but two therapists working together allowed greater freedom and support in containing this demanding group. Previously one client, who I shall call Deborah, had been seen individually for art therapy and the others had worked using art therapy in different group situations.

The setting

The art therapy department where the work took place was in a Therapeutic Core Unit for people with learning difficulties. The art room was large and light with two big windows looking over the front of the house and clients' current work was displayed on the walls. There was a choice of places to sit and work, and the art materials were easily accessible. The atmosphere of the room was friendly and inviting.

The general aim of the Unit was to help improve an individual's quality of life and to maximise possibilities for a full participation in the life of the community. The particular needs of the clients were carefully assessed and each was offered a timetable incorporating the specialist therapies most appropriate for them. The principle behind this was that people with learning difficulties share with all of us the need to enjoy a varied and stimulating week, to have a sense of identity within their community and to make friends. It was also upheld that challenges and an opportunity to experiment should be possible for everyone. Art therapy can provide encouragement to explore relationships with other people and the art materials using a new language, a language that does not need to use words, that is both accessible and stimulating.

The advantages for the clients of working in a group

People with autism tend to find themselves isolated. They often have difficulties both in communicating with and in understanding other people. In this group the members were aware of each other and interactions did occur that could be supported by the therapist. For example, one participant who I shall call Anthony had got red paint on the floor and another, who I shall call Brian, had then walked in it. A few moments later Anthony said, 'Brian's got red shoes. He's got red shoes', and laughed. Brian, a quiet character who rarely spoke, was listening and when I repeated Anthony's statement to him, he smiled broadly and seemed to enjoy the attention.

These clients seemed to benefit from interactions with other group members as well as the individual attention of the therapist. It is as though they lacked a basic inner security from which to understand complex interactions and needed encouragement from other relationships. In other words, their sense of themselves seemed so fragile that this hindered their understanding of words, signs or body language expressed by others. Even though they did not speak or interact together very much, they were interested in each other and aware of what the others in the group were doing. For example, a man I shall call Chris would start something with a material or tool that began to interest Anthony, or vice versa.

Another advantage of working with these clients in a group is that this noisy and busy atmosphere can have a supportive effect, dispelling any fear of exposure and keeping a sense of everyone working together.

The culture of the group

My first impression of working in this group was of a noisy and nearly chaotic atmosphere. The clients seemed either like demanding children craving adult attention or else very tense, defensive and highly sensitive. The noise made thinking very difficult. Anthony and Chris were very talkative and Deborah shrieked in a way that was impossible to ignore. Many things were happening at once that needed the therapists to be alert not only to the clients' individual demands but also to the group dynamics.

The clients engaged with the materials in a tactile way, which I thought was possibly related to the early stages of oral and anal development. The bottles of poster paint were used with huge enjoyment for the physical properties of the material. Thickness or liquidity, dark or light, red or yellow; each of these qualities could hold a fascination and seemed to become something more imaginative than just paint. The clay and Plasticine were explored for their softness and smoothness; for their penetrability, mouldability and their potential for transformation into a terrain, a cave or a creature. Covering a sheet of paper with a painted colour was a tangible example of one client's sense of personal power to change and transform something into something else – a blue sheet of sugar paper could become a quite different new yellow sheet.

Although there was structure and routine to the sessions, they could also vary from week to week. It only took a small shift of interest by one member to influence the rest. The situation was secure enough for us to observe influences such as the weather on a particular day, the changing seasons and individual responses to these.

The work was full of creative possibilities and I learnt from my supervisor's experience. Our coordinated thinking, which was informed by psychodynamic theory (an approach broadly based on the premise that human behaviour and relationships are shaped by conscious and unconscious influences), had the aim of promoting initiative and creativity in our clients, offering new ideas to challenge the tendency of the group members to stay safely within their own known territories. The first new initiative we introduced was to encourage the group to work together on one large sheet of paper. Another was deciding that it might be possible for the group to discuss together at the start of the session what they would like to work on that day. Although two members arrived late, we waited for them to have this discussion. My supervisor and I suggested they work on the floor for a change, but the group turned this down and decisions were taken independently as to what they would like to do. It was difficult to keep the discussion on track, but it was an interesting new step. Choice and decision making are a significant challenge for clients who rely on established habits and routines for their sense of security.

Group profile

Anthony, aged 23

Anthony was an ebullient and lively member of the group. He could speak and was repeatedly sharing his plans to 'skive off, have two dinners, go for picnics' and generally have a good time. He had an infectious laugh and was able to enjoy himself thoroughly in the art room getting up to all kinds of mischief and provoking those caring for him into having to restrain him. One of his favourite ploys was throwing items such as the washing-up liquid bottle out of the window. He could listen briefly to words restricting such activity but it did not stop him for long. In his enthusiasm Anthony seemed to be at the developmental stage of an 18-month-old toddler who would be at the height of his belief in his 'omnipotence' – a stage negotiated by all infants who learn by their experience of frustration to accept the reality principle (Rycroft, 1972).

He was often doubly incontinent during sessions, despite being reminded. It was as though he was at an arrested stage of development and because of this could not make the vital connection between the sensations in his body and the evident consequences moments later. When this happened his mood would change and he would become quieter and morose for a while.

Brian, aged 29

Brian was a quiet and undemanding person. He could speak but as a rule only answered when questioned and then only with a single quietly spoken word. He was of medium height, aware of his appearance and always looked well turned out. He had a slightly protruding lower lip and held his fingers in stiff and strange positions. When he was happy or excited about something he ran on the spot, hopping from leg to leg, tensing his arms.

When I first came to the group he was very tense, withdrawn and shy. I was in the group for about a month before any communication was made between us. He was nervous of anyone moving behind him and disliked being touched. There was a suspicion, originating from documentation about his past history, that he was sexually abused at boarding school when he was younger. If he became distressed in any way he would tense up, make a strange grimace with his mouth and bite his hand, where a callus had formed from doing so.

Chris, aged 24

Chris was very talkative and it was noticeably quiet when he was away. His speech was often hard to understand as he tended to gabble, running all his words together and leaving no gaps or pauses. His chief concerns were for his brother, about whom he talked constantly, his parents and the people who cared for him where he lived. He would make pretend phone calls to his brother and his father several times during a session.

He seemed to need and constantly seek out the therapist's attention. Another of his preoccupations was with the time. He gave the feeling that he was hardly ever able to be fully aware in the present moment and also that he was without much recourse to day-dreaming or pondering. He very often looked at his watch and made encouraging remarks about how quickly time had passed and how it would soon be 3 o'clock. He gave the impression that he did this marking of time wherever he was, constantly anticipating the next event and perhaps never enjoying the full experience of being there, now.

Deborah, aged 33

Deborah was the only female in the group. Being with such an active group of males could have deterred her from coming, but it was reported that art therapy was one of the few activities that she seemed keen to attend. She was non-verbal and communicated using a combination of Makaton signs and her own way of shrieking to gain attention. She was constantly 'twiddling' her fingers, holding first one hand then the other in front of her face. This looked as though she was shielding herself from facing other people. She also bit her hands and they were calloused as a result.

Deborah's chief preoccupation during the sessions was with drinking tea and eating biscuits. From the beginning of each session she was frequently reminding us about teatime, as though we may forget the time. She needed reassuring that the time would come. When it was teatime she would take as many biscuits as she could, and during the session we had to watch that she was not rifling through the drawers looking for them.

Week after week, Deborah would help herself to a palette and pour oceans of different colours into it, so that the paint overflowed onto the table and floor. I had the sense of a tremendous unfulfilled need in her; as though she had never been able to feel that she had had enough of anything or felt contained or satisfied as she matured. Consequently she always needed to take too much.

Deborah really enjoyed listening to tapes and would ask for music at the beginning of the group. Sometimes, for reasons we could only guess at, she would sit and cry while listening.

Edward, aged 20

Edward was the most recent member of the group to join and, unlike the others, he lived at home with his family, who had found it difficult to accept the diagnosis of autism. He used to be able to speak, and had stopped completely only eighteen months before his referral for art therapy. He was becoming depressed and losing the use of his limbs.

It was hard to persuade him to take off his coat and he spent several sessions standing for the entire time by the door and outside the door in a small lobby. He had shown an interest in switching off the electric lights and pulling the chains in the toilets.

He smiled a lot and looked excited when he arrived, but it was hard to make eye contact or to make a connection with him.

Ways of working with this group

The group ran from 1.30 to 3.00 one afternoon a week. There was an established structure of doing art work for the first hour and then ending with tea and biscuits for the last half hour. The last half hour was clearly anticipated by the clients. This demonstrated that autistic clients can understand the time frame of the sessions and, feeling secure in the structure of a routine, are able to anticipate regular events. The fact that the members of this group, except Edward, knew each other well made it easier for them to use the group situation therapeutically. The consistent and repeated pattern of each week built gradually into a familiar, creative opportunity for them. The work was long-term and slow, but not at all at a standstill; I found that slight incremental changes occurred week after week, for example, a gradual filling of the same page with intense scribbles of different colours indicating movement and progress.

The clients were not told what to do but were offered the time and the materials to use as they wanted, which was a particular opportunity for them because they were usually involved in organised group activities. They each reacted differently to our approach and while, for example, Brian would work on the same drawing for weeks on end, Chris chose to use a variety of art materials each time.

Although it is true that we allowed the group members to find their chosen art materials for themselves, I and my supervisor also talked afterwards about how each session had gone and discussed strategies for increasing each member's engagement. This client group can become stuck in the same safe, tried and tested area and could benefit from a fresh prompt if judged rightly and offered at an appropriate moment. For example, we came to a point when we wanted to make some changes and agreed a strategy. We had noticed that Anthony was using a brush with interest, that Brian had been using the same materials for weeks and Deborah had become isolated from the rest of the group. Thus there were many reasons for making a change, so we put out a large area of cartridge paper over the tables before the group arrived. We hoped this would bring the group members together to work with each other rather than each at his own activity. The reaction of the group was generally enthusiastic. Only Deborah held back and continued working as she had before. Anthony and Chris started painting immediately, and Brian, who arrived slightly later, joined in easily. Edward was unwell and was away during this period.

We repeated this first experiment of working together on one large sheet many times, and found that the larger scale could inspire a more expansive approach as well as creating more opportunities for interaction between the group members. Nothing could be forced, but having new opportunities easily available could facilitate a change of experience for these clients. New materials at the right moment could trigger curiosity or evoke a memory causing a chain of explorations. When the routine is well established and secure an intervention like this is more likely to be accepted within the group and does not appear to cause anxieties.

Figure 4.1 Group painting

A group session

There follows part of the process notes that were written straight after the session, which explains their brief note form. I decided to leave them unedited to keep the sense of liveliness in the experience.

> Brian came in after Anthony, Chris and Deborah had started. I asked if he wanted last week's drawing. He said 'Yes', so I got it down from the cupboard and he sat with it in front of him. I was sitting away from him. Shortly after, I moved over to the corner next to Brian and asked if he wanted a colour. He said 'Yes'. 'Which colour would you like?' No response. 'Would you like me to choose a colour?' 'Yes.' I chose a red and he got to work, the usual to-ing and fro-ing between looking at me and scribbling. At one point early on I went to get up. He seemed horrified, reacted very strongly, tensing and grimacing and I quickly sat down again. Brian seemed to be making contact with a very early stage of development while he was working like this. I thought he was like a dependent baby, unable to demand, searching my face for my attention and using it while scribbling intensely. If my mind wandered for too long the scribbling stopped. When I attended consistently he sometimes went into an excited spasm and scribbled more. A trust might have been developing, offering a much needed mirroring of his sense of self found in my dependable gaze. 'The infant discovers himself in the mother's response' (Wright, 2009). Lots of noise and laughter going on around us all the time.
>
> Anthony got a big chunk of blue finger paint and drew freely on the large sheet. He also painted in black scribbles with a brush. I was concentrating on the others and he had his back to me so I missed a bit and the next thing I knew he was squeezing a purple bottle of paint all over his work – great floods of paint. He had a really good time. Making jokes about skiving off, etc., amid general hilarity. He was doubly incontinent at about this time and needed to be taken out of the room and cleaned up. Later Anthony cut up and destroyed his big painting. As he did it there was a more depressed feeling about him. He put the dripping bits in the bin very deliberately. It felt important to let him experience this disposal. I had left Edward sitting and smiling, my supervisor managed to offer him paint and he set about painting masses of yellow on blue sugar paper. He got very involved and looked very pleased. It was quite magical to see him busy like that.

Despite the strain of feeling chaos could break out in any quarter – paint pouring, wetting themselves and Anthony's significant destruction of his painting – this session had a quite wonderful atmosphere of innocent enthusiasm.

The presence of my supervisor in these group sessions was a vital ingredient for containing what often appeared to me, the trainee, as chaotic and uncontained. Her calm confidence as an experienced art therapist held the whole group together.

How these clients use art therapy

Anthony

Anthony's main interest seemed to be in exploring his concerns with mess and control. He appeared to need to experience the excitement of making a mess and exploring how far he could go with it, discovering his own power to find its limits and then to restore order and destroy or dispose of what he had made.

When I first joined the group Anthony was working with clay and he had developed a routine whereby he got out the same lump each week, set it on a board and banged bits of wood into it with a rolling pin, making a Stonehenge-like structure. After some time he would then pour water over the whole thing and explore the pools of liquid clay. Finally he would take a brush and paint the table with the sludge.

One day Chris's painting spread over onto his clay and gave Anthony the idea to mix paint onto the clay base. This caused us to think of spreading out a large roll of cartridge paper to shift his established routine. We repeated this regularly and introduced Anthony to finger paints, leaving them within easy reach for him to find – later he would look for them himself. Initially he got out lumps of the paint using a paintbrush handle but he moved on to using his hands and making marks directly onto the page. Then he started to use the poster paints, squeezing whole bottles of paint out onto the page or into a pot, one colour onto another.

He would also experiment with other substances such as washing-up liquid and scouring cream. One week he poured a bottle and a half of lemon squash down the sink, before we realised what was happening. Sometimes he would eat the paint and drink the paint water, perhaps confusing what they were or perhaps experimenting. The mess was extraordinary and although it was exciting, it was also alarming. I thought that he was using these substances to negotiate his way in an early stage of his development connected to his incontinence and inability to control this.

As teatime approached, Anthony would try hard to clear up his area and put things away as best he could. This activity seemed to be an important part of the whole process of his work in the art room. In time Anthony became more interactive and willing to try to speak to us about his problems than he had been before.

It was interesting for me to note my automatic reactions while sitting next to someone who is pouring paint everywhere. I felt panic initially: was chaos about to engulf us, was it a waste of the precious materials, and who was going to clear it all up? Counterbalancing this was the obvious need the client had to experience this and the realisation that the materials were there for just this purpose. Anthony had benefited from being allowed to find his own way and I had survived the tension between chaos and order.

Brian

When I first joined the group Brian had a long-term routine of having a lump of clay in front of him and a pot of water. He would touch the clay repeatedly with a wetted finger, smoothing the top, sometimes reaching inside the plastic bag but usually with the clay out on a board. It appeared to be a sensual, comforting activity and he would continue until his clay was put away till the next week. It was a period when both he and Deborah seemed rather stuck. We had discussed whether both these clients might leave the group.

When we introduced the large piece of paper, he joined in using a roller, with Anthony and Chris painting enthusiastically beside him. He spoke more than usual and allowed me to wash his face at the end.

At about this time I attended his Life Plan Meeting and heard how well he was doing and how his medication was being reduced. Although the next week he went back to his clay, the following week he started to draw. After this I gradually developed a closer relationship with him when he began to scribble looking back to me directly, searching my eyes as he worked. I tried to return his gaze as genuinely and receptively as possible and it was as though he drank it in.

I thought that the scribbling indicated an affirmation of self for which he needed this attention from me. It was like a child acquiring a sense of himself through his mother's constant attentiveness and it seemed to be necessary for his development. He seemed very aware of me, and without any signs or outward demands, I could sense that he wanted my attention. I have rarely had such a focused, intense, wordless interchange with anyone.

Figure 4.2 Brian's drawing after ten sessions

After the Easter break we were working together as usual and he suddenly hit me smartly on the back. I questioned him, surprised, as to whether this was because I had been away. 'Yes, sorry – sorry,' he replied. During my third to last session with the group, I had to announce that I was going to leave soon. It was difficult for me to do this, and with Brian I felt a sense of betrayal. However, the parting was successfully managed by speaking clearly with Brian about what he might be feeling during the last few sessions. I was also helped in my own supervision to see how part of the problem arose from my own personal experience of partings.

Chris

Chris was the only member of the group who worked figuratively and he used the paint freely. He produced many paintings in one session and he named what he was doing, for example calling out, 'It's a ship!' A few moments later the same image became an aeroplane, then a person.

Chris always seemed to be in the present moment and in touch with a vivid imaginative world. For example, he scribbled a line with a felt tip that represented one of the people who looked after him where he lived. He then cut the image in half and looked really worried that he had damaged one of them, saying, 'Oh no, I've cut Mary in half'. It transpired that he was cross with her for going away, but hadn't meant to go so far.

He spoke frequently about his brother John, who was good to Chris, but who was also the cause of Chris's jealousy. He would announce that there were two Johns. My supervisor explored this with him suggesting that he didn't always like his brother who could sometimes be annoying. Referring to Kleinian thinking she stated that 'There is one John who you like and one John who you don't like so much. Really they are the same person'. This clarification using a psychodynamic approach was clearly understood by Chris and soon after this he said, 'I feel much better today'.

I discovered by chance how well Chris responded to play-acting. He came over to me complaining of a sore arm. I pretended to be a doctor and bandaged him up – he enjoyed this enormously. The next week he pretended that he was the doctor. Then he pretended that he was John and found it very funny when I played along. This play-acting occurred when Chris was less well and unable to concentrate, so not getting as much out of his art work as he had before. It could be that this sort of play was less demanding on his fine motor skills and concentration.

Deborah

When I first met Deborah her habit was to accept help pinning papers to a board and then to help herself to huge quantities of paint. Using a paint brush she would cover areas of the paper with colour and one week she painted four such double paintings. Sometimes she seemed very absorbed in this activity and would sing and talk to herself in her own wordless way while working.

We tried to integrate Deborah more closely with the group when we decided to try a joint painting using a large roll of cartridge paper. The first time we did this Deborah was very reticent and so we put some paper up in her usual place, but she didn't touch this either. The next week we tried to persuade her to join the others at the table but she insisted on working at her usual place. The week following this she did sit at the table and scribbled with the pens, which we rolled across to her. Unfortunately, later on in the session, Anthony came and painted in Deborah's area. I protested, but she showed no signs of minding and seemed more concerned about tea and biscuit time.

As time went by Deborah became less involved in her art work. She would sit at the table, but spent more of her time going to the toilet or sitting twiddling her fingers and listening to tapes, checking every so often that we hadn't forgotten about teatime. I felt guilty about Deborah because I knew that she would have benefited from more attention and it was partly because she was not as demanding as the rest of the group that she was neglected. This had possibly been an often-repeated experience for her all her life and was perhaps a situation she had come to expect.

Eventually we thought to get out an easel for Deborah so that she could paint in an upright position again. She responded well and did more work than she had done in the previous month.

Edward

Edward could be a disruptive influence on the group. He attended five sessions and then missed the following five sessions, so that he lost the confidence he had gained and could no longer trust the situation. For the last few of the sessions he attended, he stood by the door and periodically escaped out of it, leaving it open so that other people passing by would look in, thus upsetting the security of the group.

The usual solution to this problem would be to make it clear to the client that it was fine to go out of the room briefly but a prolonged absence meant that they must leave and go home.

However, we thought that Edward wanted to stay. The look on his face was excited and interested, but it seemed he didn't quite dare. He managed to keep himself in a very powerful position, monopolising the attention of one of the therapists for the whole session.

Before the unfortunate break in sessions, Edward did manage to do some all-over colour paintings and showed considerable enjoyment in doing them. It would have been an important step for him if he had dared to stay, but other aspects of his life beyond the art therapy room were causing difficulties for those caring for him and so they were not getting him to the Unit.

Conclusion

Although this was a short period in the life of the group, I gradually got to know a lot about the participants and saw them change. This group evolved considerably during the time I was with them.

Usually the main emphasis is on training such clients in aspects of behaviour and basic education. Art therapy offers them a special and different opportunity encouraging initiative, spontaneity and autonomy. Unlike the more directive forms of instruction that give information to be learned in a situation more like the classroom at school, the non-directive nature of art therapy gives an active role to the participant. Within the continuity of the known framework, confidence can be fostered and visible progress made.

Ideal conditions are a physical space that has enough room and light for comfortable working, with running water and circumstances that can withstand considerable mess. It is also important that the door can be closed and the session is not interrupted so that the group members can feel as safe and relaxed as possible in a stable, calm and familiar environment in order to lower psychological defences, which can then promote creativity, well-being and understanding.

Generally the group came enthusiastically and were able to use the art materials without direction from the therapists. I experienced a sense of freedom in the art room, of clients being allowed to do whatever they wanted or nothing at all, which I thought was one of the most valuable aspects of art therapy. There were a variety of materials waiting to be tried, and the therapist was available all the time in the background, providing a non-coercive, supportive presence.

This client group demands qualities of calm, patient attentiveness from the therapist, and a willingness to watch carefully and consider how each member works, in relation to the dynamic of the whole group. The chaos could be taxing but work was done and gentle suggestions from the therapists facilitated fresh connections for the group members.

Continuity week to week was managed by on-going review and discussion between the therapists. In the heat of the session so much happened that afterwards the therapists needed to feed back to each other in order to gather a more objective view. Through this discussion new initiatives could be considered in the interest of the whole group.

I gained enormously from working with this group and learned much about the different ways that art therapy can be used. I saw that art materials could become transformative substances offering the opportunity to make a personal expression and I witnessed how using them could support such fragile early stages of development.

Afterword

My original Clinical Training Study provided me with a formative experience in my career as an art therapist. Although I never again worked with clients diagnosed with such severe autistic features, it has become clear that the various identified characteristics listed on the autistic spectrum can be recognised in more able clients. Many young children have autistic qualities in, for example, sequencing, timing and coordination, which they either grow out of or learn to cope with in time. I contend that we all have areas of our functioning that could be called mildly autistic. It is a sliding scale of difficulties of which this group showed the more extreme and disabling examples. It was a valuable training for me, to work with clients who displayed such very early stages of development, alerting me to the more primitive and hidden insecurities present in us all.

Working from a psychodynamic theoretical perspective remains at the foundation of my work as a therapist. Experience of working in this way has developed my sensitivity to the particular needs of each individual client, allowing them as much space and freedom as possible to compensate for the inevitable imbalance of power in our different roles (Rees, 1998). As was shown in this group, there is often a need both for empowering the client with the freedom to choose and making a carefully considered suggestion at the right moment.

Both the method of working together with another therapist in a group and the theoretical objectives expressed in the study continue to be relevant in my practice. It has been the model for the many children's groups I later facilitated with an art therapy trainee as a co-facilitator.

This training experience forms the foundation of my conviction in the efficacy of working non-directively in art therapy group work.

References

Rees, M. (1998) 'Frames of reference' in Rees, M. (ed.), *Drawing on Difference*, Hove Routledge.
Rycroft, C. (1972) *A Critical Dictionary of Psychoanalysis*, London: Penguin.
Wright, K. (2009) *The Search for Form: Mirroring and Attunement*, Hove: Routledge.

Chapter 5

Rhythm and flow

Re-thinking art therapy with an autistic young man

Angela Byers

Introduction

This chapter investigates the way I worked with an autistic young man for several years when he had art therapy with me. At the time there were different theories about the causes of autism, some saying that it is the result organic failure and others that it is due to very early psychological trauma. I took my approach from psychoanalytic thinking and I have elaborated on it in this chapter. Psychoanalytic theory allowed me to think about ways of working with my client and also offered me a way of containing my own anxieties.

In this chapter I describe the pre-symbolic mode in Ogden's theory of the 'autistic-contiguous position' (1992) and then I write briefly about Winnicott's theory of 'holding' (1965) and Bion's theory of containment (1962), particularly as explained by Ogden in a later paper (2004). I introduce Christopher and make connections with the content of his art therapy sessions; I record excerpts from my clinical notes to show examples that prompted my thinking, and finally I draw the themes together in a conclusion.

Theoretical background

In his book *The Primitive Edge of Experience*, Ogden (1992) gives the label 'autistic-contiguous position' to the 'primitive, pre-symbolic, sensory-dominated mode' that he says precedes Klein's 'paranoid-schizoid' and 'depressive positions' in the development of an infant. Ogden (1992) uses the term 'mode' and adds that 'each of the three modes' 'represents a pole of dialectical process between which experience is generated' (1992: 77). They complement each other, so that a person can move between them.

In this first stage of life the infant has no cognitive awareness of himself as a separate entity, although he is capable of feeling sensations and directing himself towards them, for example responding to light and sound. In Ogden's autistic-contiguous position anything that is experienced makes an impression, which is described by Ogden as a 'sensory impression' (Ogden, 1992).

Impressions are made through touch, sight, sound, smell and sensations felt within the body. The infant, being helpless, is usually looked after by his mother, who holds him, looks at him and talks to him. As time progresses rhythms fall into place, for example feeding, nappy changing, and cuddling happen at increasingly predictable times. The sensed features of outside objects become familiar, features such as shapes, colours, sounds and smells of elements in the environment, including bodies. Whilst the infant feels the edges of things again and again against his skin, he develops a growing sense of 'boundedness', of being within his skin.

Some infants become so anxious that they are unable to experience this process. They cannot feel that their bodies are 'bounded' or held in and they are terrified of dissolving into nothingness. Instead they retreat into autistic defences or pathological autism itself.

Tustin (1992) describes how the autistic infant has withdrawn from the process of learning to relate to others, into an 'encapsulated' system designed to protect the infant from what it fears. Autistic people find 'autistic sensation objects' (Tustin, 1992) that are within their control and provide sensations that make them feel stronger and calmer in the face of potential panic. These objects may be physical like a stone, or may be a product of the mind, such as ritualised language (Tustin, 1992).

Ogden (1992) says that it is not possible to internalise the mother in the autistic-contiguous position because the infant has no sense of an internal space. However, the infant can begin to be aware of his mother as separate by feeling her shape against his own shape, through his skin. An adult with some autistic symptoms can begin to experience his therapist as another person through imitation of her 'shape', copying what she says and does. Thus he experiences her different 'shape' whilst ensuring that she does not make a hole through his skin with her interventions.

However, Ogden adds that a pathologically autistic person will imitate in a different way, through repeating the 'shape' of the other's words in a ritualistic or 'deadened' fashion. Such repetition is used to obstruct the other and keep them at a distance.

Winnicott's (1965) theory of holding testifies to the significance of the mother's way of touching her baby as she handles it, with an emphasis on the mother's state of mind as she attunes herself to the infant, building up a sense of 'continuity' within time, through the rhythms made when attending to body functions in day to night to day and so on. Thus the mother gives herself up to her infant, starting from where it is and bringing it into man-made time gradually and not catastrophically. At the same time the infant feels the edges of itself as its mother touches it and it touches her, and very gradually it takes on a sense of being a separate entity. This heals the sense of leaking in the autistic-contiguous position described by Ogden in 1992, and in a later paper (2004) he brings our attention to the significance of time within Winnicott's theory of holding.

In this paper Ogden differentiates between Winnicott's theory of holding and Bion's theory of container-contained. Bion's theory (1962) concerns the mental processes that lead to the ability to think. The act of containing involves the processing of unconscious 'sense impressions' (the contained) using unconscious, pre-conscious and conscious thinking to give meaning to them. The mother performs the act of containing when she ponders and thinks about her experiences of her infant, acting on her understanding by feeding it, making it more comfortable and so on. In healthy development the baby gradually internalises the process so that it can be a container for itself. The process of 'container-contained' is replicated in psychoanalysis and psychodynamic psychotherapies when the therapist ponders and thinks about her experience of the client and reacts through her behaviour and interventions.

Christopher

Christopher (a pseudonym) had weekly art therapy sessions with me in an art therapy centre. He was brought by care workers, who then left and returned after an hour. Christopher had difficulties adapting to time patterns that were imposed by other people and which he may well have experienced as impingements on his internal world. Consequently he made it difficult for his care workers to bring him on time for his session and he would often refuse to leave when the hour was over.

Christopher could use words to describe objects and events, but he was unable to construct full sentences or express abstract concepts. He was not aggressive but he expressed his frustration loudly, biting himself and pushing any obstruction out of the way even if it was a person. Therefore we had to find ways of managing him without unduly frustrating him. We had to adapt to him, like the mother of a newly born infant has to adapt to it and manage time for it.

He would use art materials in a similar way every week, although there would be gradual changes over time. It was as though there was a ritual to the use of each type of material, and when he had run out of the material or had finished that ritual, he would pause. At this point he would sometimes run out of the room, looking for his care workers, or for a toilet. It seemed that the ending of a ritual was intolerable if he could not start something else straight away and it was probably experienced as a 'hole'.

Christopher talked about art therapy at other times during the week and he would often run to get to the session. Once inside the room he would frequently lunge excitedly towards the materials, so we could see that he liked the experience. He used up all the liquid paints available and squashed oil pastels until they were finished. He would also spend a lot of time at the sink, filling it with water so that it would have overflowed if I had not taken the plug out.

He would pour paint from the bottles into little mixing pots until they overflowed, sometimes dripping it over a pot's edge, and he would watch it with fascination. He would then pour paint from the pots and the bottles onto his paper and spread it with a paintbrush. He would go over the edge of the paper and turn the sheet over so that he could paint the other side. Sometimes the finished creations would take several days to dry. It seemed that edges were significant to him and that he needed to destroy them by spreading the paint over them.

When he had squashed the oil pastels he would scratch through the marks with his nails. He did the same with the marks he made with wax crayons. It seemed that he wanted to feel the hard surface of the table underneath his drawings, the edge of the table's flat shape.

There were periods when he drew outlines, seeming to enjoy the movement of making big circles or becoming absorbed in small shapes and the quality of the lines that delineated them. At these times he worked with entities that were separate from each other.

Although interaction with Christopher was basically on his terms, he did not seem to be completely 'encapsulated'. I would try to link the metaphors suggested by his behaviour and his images with bodily processes and thought processes. For example, I would link water flowing over the edge of the sink to his resistance to finishing at the end of a session. My words were a form of reflecting out loud, in which I described the links that I had made in order to show that I was actively listening and trying to contain his expressions. He would usually ignore me but sometimes he would smile, prompt me to continue, and occasionally he would stop and look at me.

He also showed an awareness of loss. His behaviour would change in the session after someone significant to him had left him, for example he would talk less and make sounds that I thought were sad. He appeared to enjoy his interactions with others, even though they were ritualistic and on his own terms, and it seemed that he missed those others when they were not there.

Managing Christopher

My first encounter with Christopher was overwhelming. We were in a large art room with a lot of paint available that did not belong to me. I was anxious about the quantities of paint that he used and I did not know how to manage the session with someone who reacted to confrontation with such frustration. I found it hard to think in a containing way.

I decided to use practical means to manage Christopher's sessions. I found a smaller room and gave him limited quantities of paint, paper and oil pastels, renewing them every week. I now established my own limits and this made it possible for me to think about our experiences within his sessions.

Christopher would start his sessions in a state of excitement, but would become calmer as he became absorbed in the sensations of using the materials. At these times I would feel pleasantly sleepy. Ogden says that the analyst or therapist working with an autistic patient often experiences 'a rather pleasant feeling of being suspended between sleep and wakefulness', like reverie but sensory dominated (1992: 44–5).

When Christopher paused at the end of an activity, I would sometimes suggest another medium that I anticipated he would like to use, in order to keep him in the room and involved in art therapy. It can be likened to prompting the infant to feed when it becomes distracted.

It was difficult to finish Christopher's art therapy sessions. I would try to prepare him by warning him that it was fifteen, ten and then five minutes to the ending. Eventually I developed a plan in which I removed the materials and left the room, to wait in the corridor with his care workers until Christopher had grown tired of what he was doing. Thus we introduced reality without forcing him to come out until he was ready.

Holding

Art therapy was full of sensual experiences for Christopher. Paint and water flowed and could be felt on the skin, oil pastels could be smeared and drawings could be scraped and scratched. Colour could be separated or mixed, lines drawn in curves or jaggedly. His finished images were often beautiful in their sensuousness.

He brought rituals that ordered time in familiar ways and he pulled me into his rituals when he could. I would try to manage our time together as smoothly as I could.

He experienced literal impressions when he pushed on the surface of the paper and mental impressions when I talked to him with my own words or suggested another activity. Whilst he could control his own actions, he could not control mine and the demand to leave a session before he was ready was experienced by him as intrusive into his sense of time.

Christopher would repeat words over and over loudly until I felt it as an intrusion into my world. I found that he would relax if I repeated them back and I think he wanted a reaction from me, to see if I could feel his shape. When I described some of his processes he would urge me to repeat my descriptions, thus feeling the shape of what I said about his shape.

Container-contained

The art therapist observes her client manipulating materials and reacting to what happens. The therapist muses and tries to make sense of what her client is doing. Whilst Christopher manipulated the materials, some of his actions and words gradually made sense to me, in terms of bodily functions linked to functions of the mind.

His love of unbounded flow was pertinent to Ogden's autistic-contiguous position (1992). He would pour paint slowly over the edges of pots, he would try to let water overflow over the edge of the sink and he would paint over the edge of the paper. I likened this to playing with the edges of the session, the beginning and ending that he found so hard to accept as well as the demands of other people, and I would express such thoughts out loud. Occasionally Christopher would then show his interest by smiling, prompting me to repeat what I was saying and occasionally stopping and staring at me.

At such times I wanted to believe that his interest meant that he could connect with the content of what I was saying, or that he would feel my attempts to make sense of his behaviour and thus experience some containment.

Countertransference

I often felt afraid whilst I waited for Christopher's session because I feared his unpredictability and my lack of control over his actions and I think I was thus sensing the autistic-contiguous fear of unboundedness. But during his sessions I switched between alert attentiveness and reverie, often feeling warm towards him, as someone who was not entirely encapsulated and who did react to me, as when he would ask me to repeat what I said, or when he stopped and looked at me.

After his sessions I would feel impatient and angry over the amount of time it took to clear up Christopher's mess, and over the exhaustion of having been with him. Several times I hit my head accidentally on a shelf that was over the sink and this would release my fury at what could be compared to the 'tyranny' of the autistic client that Ogden (1992) says is felt by the analyst or therapist.

Thus I experienced something of the intensity of 'sensation-dominated experience' (Ogden, 1992: 52) in my countertransference.

Clinical illustrations

I have taken excerpts from my notes describing parts of sessions that show the origins of my thoughts and ideas.

Session 127: skin, overflow and edges

Christopher used the paints, washed up some pots and returned to painting a few times. When he washed I noticed that he was rubbing his hands and arms a lot and I commented that he was cleaning his skin. I became concerned that he might let the water overflow, so I commented that the water was running, it might overflow, but I added that his skin held his body in, and his mind held his thoughts.

Later he drew big circles that filled the page, feeling the hardness of the surface by pressing with his pen.

In this session he experienced the flow of paint and water and also felt the 'edges' of his arms and the table. I linked this to thinking and hoped that he would experience my thoughtfulness about what he was doing.

Session 131: I ease the transition to another activity

Christopher burst into the room with enthusiasm. He painted and then washed, going backwards and forwards between the table and the sink several times for about twenty-five minutes. He covered the paper with paint and folded it over to give himself more space to paint on. Then he squashed the oil pastels and went to wash his hands.

I arranged some fresh paper during this break in his activities and when he came back to the table he picked up the pens and drew with enthusiasm.

Session 134: different rhythms

Christopher painted for a while and seemed to be watching the different kinds of strokes he made. After this he washed the pots, but then he did not go back to the materials. He said 'Peter' (the name of his care worker) and went to the door. I persuaded him to come back. Later he went out of the door and stood in the corridor looking stunned. He said 'David' (the name of another care worker).

I explained that they were not coming yet and that we had a lot more of art therapy left, but he came in and said, 'Bye bye, art therapy'.

I said 'I think you want to finish now and you don't want to stay, but we have to because David and Peter aren't here yet'. He settled down to using wax crayons and became involved with what he was doing.

Session 160: negotiating the end of the paint and of painting

Christopher started the session by talking a lot. He smiled and this caused me to smile and to feel good.

Then he used a lot of paint and increased its extent by adding water with his brush. He folded the paper over and, as it was soggy, he was able to mould it round the jar of water.

After a long time he looked for more paint, even trying to open a locked cupboard. I said, 'You want more paint, but it's gone'. He came and sat facing me and I commented that he might have been thinking about the fact that it had all gone and that perhaps this was sad. After a pause I said that he could choose what to do next, but he still looked for paint and managed to get some out of the bottom of a bottle.

He walked out of the room and stood outside. It took a long time to persuade him to go back into the room.

However, he went back to manipulating the paint already on his painting and when it was time to finish, he did not want to leave.

Session 175: holidays and gaps in the session

Christopher said 'holiday' and I acknowledged that Peter was going on holiday next week, that we had art therapy next week and the week after, but that I would be going away in the week after that.

After some painting he worked at the sink, filling bottles and just about keeping the water from splashing everywhere. He moaned, 'uuuuurh', and it sounded as though he was in a trance so I commented that it seemed to be soothing.

He came back to the table and sat. Then he left the room and stood outside the door and eventually he came back. I sat with him and commented that this was a gap, which was like a sort of change. He got up and filled in the blank bits of paper on his painting. He said 'gap' and I said 'like you felt a gap' and he asked me to move the painting away.

Summary

In these excerpts Christopher covered paper with paint, spread the paint over the edges, folded the paper and painted on the other side. He filled containers with water and made fountains under the tap. He felt their surfaces when he washed the containers and he felt his skin when he cleaned the paint off of himself. Similarly he felt the hardness of the table when he squashed the oil pastels and drew with pens. Sometimes he soothed himself and created autistic shapes and sometimes he pressed hard as if to emphasise the boundary of his skin and create an autistic object.

I made links between concrete objects and the human body and mind. Often he did not respond to what I said, but sometimes he did, as when he filled in the blanks on his paper after I had talked about gaps. I responded to him in various ways: sometimes I regulated the flow of water; sometimes I followed his instructions; sometimes I told him what I thought was going on. For example when I showed him that I recognised his difficulty, in session 134, he settled down and it seemed that my recognition was soothing to him, as though I could feel his shape.

Christopher's own rhythms did not necessarily correspond to the beginnings and endings of his sessions. When he had finished an activity and could not move on to another one, he would often leave the room and look stunned as though faced with 'nothing'. Conversely, he would continue painting when it was time to leave. He was also affected when the regularity of his weekly sessions was interrupted.

Conclusion

The autistic person has an encapsulated system that is used to protect him from infringement by others, and he obtains reassurance through contact with autistic objects (Tustin, 1992). Christopher sought sensations from handling art materials and water, he sought the feel of edges and the predictable, ritualistic rhythms of his words and his activities, and he obtained reassurance from these autistic objects. He often left the room when there was a gap at the end of a sequence, as though he was running away from potential panic. I had to attune myself to Christopher in order to keep his rhythms going smoothly within the time boundaries of the session. Occasionally he showed a hint of interest in my 'shape' by responding to what I said.

My reflections were the result of my musings, when I was trying to contain his 'sense impressions' through unconscious, pre-conscious and conscious thinking. I hoped to have an effect on Christopher through the act of telling him about the connections I had made, when the act of telling him was more significant than the content of what I said. I worked experientially, rather than through interpretation, and I was not hoping to cure Christopher of his autism but wanted to provide a containing, structured experience.

I have presented a construct that enabled me to progress with Christopher's art therapy. Ogden's theory of the austistic-contiguous position (1992) and Tustin's observations of encapsulation and autistic objects (1992) have enabled me to give meaning to Christopher's behaviour. Ogden's (1992), Winnicott's (1965) and Bion's (1962) observations and theories have helped me to think about my approach as Christopher's art therapist, whilst Ogden's paper (2004) has helped me to clarify some of the differences between 'holding' and 'container-contained'.

Afterword

In my chapter I explain something of Ogden's 'autistic-contiguous position' (1992), which he observed in some of his patients without pathological autism and who were in psychoanalysis with him. They experienced a sense of leaking, an inability to stop sensations flowing through the body/mind.

Rostron (2010) describes 'too many sensations at once' and I suggest that this is another way of putting such a feeling into words. Thus Christopher's preoccupation with flow and edges can be understood as connected to these unbounded sensations and I think that he was trying to get away from his feeling of panic produced by a pause in his involvement with soothing activities, which served as autistic objects (Tustin, 1992).

When writing this chapter I referred to Ogden (1992) and Winnicott (1965) to describe how the mother/caregiver responds to the infant and develops rhythms over time which become predictable; then to Bion (1962) who explains how the mother gives the infant experiences of containment when she tries to understand what sensations he is experiencing and when she responds to them.

Winnicott, Bion and Ogden developed their theories from the clinical material presented in psychoanalysis and Winnicott also used material he observed in his practice as a paediatrician. Some years later than Winnicott and Bion, Stern (1985) made detailed observations of infants and mothers in his experimental research and he pointed out that infants cannot experience exactly what had been described in psychoanalysis because they are unable to symbolise. Stern's theories and those of other contemporaries influenced Ogden, who formulated an autistic-contiguous pre-symbolic mode.

Evans and Dubowski (2001) are also influenced by Stern and advocate careful and detailed art therapy assessments for people with autistic spectrum symptoms in order to look for the cues that the client makes. This enables the art therapist to plan how she will respond to her clients during their art therapy, in order to achieve 'attunement', which is significant because, as Rostron (2010) comments, attunement produces a physical change in the brain. Attunement leads to interaction and therefore the theory of 'intersubjectivity' becomes significant and Bragge and Fenner (2009) describe how they adapted this theory to interact with an autistic client through the art materials themselves.

I did not know about these theories when I worked with Christopher and I did not join in with the art making. He enacted his preoccupation with flow and edges and as a result he enjoyed art therapy and showed that it mattered to him. Thus it added to his quality of life, to his 'well-being'.

If I were to work with him now I would follow the guidance of Evans and Dubowski (2001) and observe him elsewhere, in the company of people who were familiar to him, and I would consider using video recording to help me to find his cues to interpersonal relating. Although there were times when Christopher stopped and looked at me after an intervention I had made and it is likely that these were indeed moments of attunement, I think they were a surprise to both of us. It may be that there could have been more such moments, which could then have been developed further had I been more aware of what to look for. Perhaps this would have enhanced my work with Christopher.

References

Bion, W. (1962) *Learning from Experience*, London: Karnac Books.
Bragge, A. and Fenner, P. (2009) 'The emergence of the "Interactive Square" as an approach to art therapy with children on the autistic spectrum', *The International Journal of Art Therapy: Inscape*, 14 (1): 17–28.
Evans, K. and Dubowski, J. (2001) *Art Therapy with Children on the Autistic Spectrum*, London and Philadelphia: Elizabeth Kingsley.
Ogden, T. (1992) *The Primitive Edge of Experience*, London: Karnac Books.
—— (2004) 'On holding and containing, being and dreaming', *The International Journal of Psychoanalysis*, 85 (6): 1349–64.
Rostron, J. (2010) 'Amodal perception and language in art therapy with autism', *The International Journal of Art Therapy: Inscape*, 15 (1): 36–49.
Stern, D. (1985) *The Interpersonal Life of the Human Infant*, New York: Basic Books.
Tustin, F. (1992) *Autistic States in Children*, revised edition, London: Routledge.
Winnicott, D.W. (1965) *The Maturational Processes and the Facilitating Environment*, London: Karnac.

Chapter 6

Images and imagination

A Jungian approach to art therapy with an autistic woman

Alison Goldsmith

This is an account of art therapy work with a woman in her fifties. Sessions were held in a residential home once a week over a period of four years.

Impairment of imaginative activity is one of the chief diagnostic criteria for autism (Frith 1999); imagination is also a key concept in Jungian and post-Jungian theory and practice. The term *imagination* is often used pejoratively to call into question the veracity of something that cannot be evidenced when, for example, someone is accused of 'imagining the whole thing'.

I use the term *image* in the context of this work to refer to actual images, or drawings, but also in the sense of an 'inner image' or idea (Jung, 1921: para. 743). The inner images and ideas in this chapter are mostly the products of my own imagination or fantasy which Jung held to be 'the chief mark of the artistic mentality' (Jung, 1921: para. 720). It will become apparent from the following account that I rely heavily on my own imagination to guide me through the work.

Symbolic representation is another capacity that is impaired in autism but central to the work of the creative artist who, through his imagination, transforms his materials into images and artefacts that convey his ideas and hold more meaning than the original elemental substance of the raw materials alone. The realised image or artefact is symbolic in the sense that it represents something other than itself. For Jung the artist was more than a 'reproducer of appearances' (1921: para. 720), he was a creator, and the symbolic images the artist created were not only symptomatic of his current psychological state but were purposeful in that they 'adumbrate lines of future development' (1921: para. 720). Jung held that the symbol has a *transcendent function* in bridging a gap between the real and the imaginary, the rational and irrational and consequently the gulf between our inner and outer worlds (Jung, 1917, 1960). In art therapy both the artefact, whether it is an image or a three dimensional object, and the process, facilitated by the presence of the therapist and the substance of the materials, constitutes a third area not only between imagination and reality but also between the therapist and the client.

As art therapists, our professional identity is intimately bound up with the materials; in offering them to our clients we are offering something valuable, something of ourselves. They may not always be traditional art materials and can include found objects and other items, for example the account given by Halliday of her client's use of a typewriter and blackboard (Halliday, 1978) and my client's use of cellophane, described later in this chapter. Transformation of the raw materials into symbolic artefacts can be facilitated through a playful approach in which the client is open to their plasticity and unpredictability, a creative process that requires imagination on the part of both client and therapist.

In the early art therapy sessions described in this chapter it was hard to imagine how the art materials could ever be used creatively and symbolically by my client, who swung between compliance, using them in a rigid and well-rehearsed way, and outright rejection when she was too disturbed to engage with me or the materials. My professional identity as an art therapist and commitment to a Jungian theoretical orientation were hard to sustain. The following is an account of a mutual process of adaptation in which my client and I were both able to relinquish some of our established ways of being and experience a more meaningful exchange.

My client, who I shall refer to as Margaret, was a woman in her mid fifties with a diagnosis of autism whose symptoms had been present from childhood. She was living in a residential home when I began work with her but had spent many years of her adult life in psychiatric hospitals. Her first admission was in her early teens and among the treatments she subsequently received was insulin coma therapy, a practice of giving increased doses of insulin daily until hypoglycaemic coma occurred, a treatment for schizophrenia later superseded by ECT. These early interventions, at a time of transition from childhood to adulthood, must have had a traumatic impact on Margaret's subsequent development. I am not suggesting that autism is the result of trauma, although Michael Fordham (one of my sources) does begin with this premise. The question that interests me is not one of aetiology but the fact that the symptoms and pathology associated with autism share common ground with those resulting from trauma and that, for the autistic person, their early experience in infancy and continuing experience of the outside world can be traumatic. My first concern was not to cure my client but to build trust and establish a way of relating to her without compounding and perpetuating this sense of trauma and consequently becoming associated with the persecutory nature of her psychological processes.

Among her symptoms, so typical of autism, were gaze avoidance, age inappropriate appearance, adherence to non-functional routines and rituals, insistence on sameness and distress over changes in routine, an unreasonable fear of falling, impaired imaginative activity and a confused sense of her body boundary and image. These autistic traits were manifest in her behaviour and appearance, which, despite her mature years, was quite childlike; her drawings too were like those of a child's early attempts at 'self and other' representations (Figure 6.1). She was seldom able to move from one room to another without an elaborate routine of touching various objects along the way. In times of stress if she could not avoid eye contact she would grimace at the other person in response to their gaze. Margaret did not easily engage in conversation with other residents in the home and the extent of her playful activity were attempts to involve others in a rigid and repetitive game of I-spy or playing the same tunes repeatedly on a small keyboard.

Another important feature was that Margaret sometimes attributed her emotional state to her 'voices', a symptom more commonly associated with schizophrenia, but Margaret's voices had a different quality from those I had experienced in my previous work with schizophrenic patients. I wondered if she had acquired a vocabulary during her early years in institutions and her voices, rather than being auditory hallucinations, were a concept, a means of shaping and naming her affect. It is worth remembering that Margaret's symptoms were present from childhood and she grew up at a time when autism was still referred to as 'childhood schizophrenia'.

Figure 6.1 Two figures touching

Margaret's mother had been concerned about her daughter from early infancy when she realised that her play activity was very repetitive and, like many other parents of autistic children, had gone to great lengths to seek help. I had been asked to work with Margaret because she was unable to attend a day centre, finding it too overwhelming and consequently becoming disruptive. We met once a week for an hour.

I first met Margaret during a preliminary meeting with the manager of the home to discuss the practicalities and possibility of art therapy. Margaret came into the meeting carrying a teddy bear and sat down in a bouncy way. Although she said very little she made it clear through her body language and presence and by positioning herself between me and the manager that she wanted to meet me and to be included in the discussion. Although the initial impression she gave was quite buoyant it was hard for her to sustain this persona, which she presented as a coping strategy. This persona, or false self, was in marked contrast with the fragility of her real self which was easily overwhelmed and invaded by the outside world.

The first session had a stilted formality about it and also a fragile sense of boundary and space. We had to meet in the chintzy communal day room because the more suitable room, the kitchen, was being decorated. We shared the room with the house cat and were also interrupted by another resident who was curious to see the new art therapist. During this first session Margaret obliged me with some perfunctory drawings before engaging me in a game of I-spy.

The drawings she made in these early sessions were simple, linear representations of objects. Schaverien describes such images as *diagrammatic* pictures in which 'the initial motivation for the picture is to tell something already consciously known' (Schaverien, 1992: 86). She mostly drew disembodied, external objects, items of clothing (clothes were important to her) or packages and parcels representing gifts that she had been given, drawing just the outer package and not the contents. Although I was not excited by her images I was impressed by the fact that, during our first rather polite and public meeting, Margaret managed to tell me about her less socially acceptable side by saying, 'I sometimes scream, you know'. It wasn't long before I experienced this for myself.

In the first few months the pattern of the sessions was either characterised by the rigid formality that I have just described or its antithesis when Margaret was in a state of acute distress, unable to leave her own room and giving clear indications that she was not prepared to engage with me. She would clutch her teddy and close her eyes on seeing me at the door of her room while shaking her head vigorously. On these occasions I would withdraw to a vacant room on the opposite side of the hallway and remain there with the door open so that I could hear her and she could see me if she chose to. I would tell her I was there if she wanted me. I could hear her inside her room; often she would be shouting, slapping her face and blowing loud, angry raspberries. I would let her know when there were ten minutes left of our allocated time together and would also tell her at the end of the time that I was leaving and, most importantly, that I would return next week.

At these times I felt self-conscious about the fact that I was sitting apparently doing nothing when I was supposed to be engaging Margaret in meaningful activity, although the staff at the home were never critical or judgemental towards me over this. It was my own inner judgemental voice I was experiencing. I felt de-skilled and that my professional identity and integrity were under question. An image came into mind of me offering a starving refugee art materials when what they really needed first and foremost was food and shelter. I think the appearance of this image in my mind resonated with a very early infant state of discomfort that Margaret may have been experiencing. It was a bodily discomfort, in fact a lack of body and sense of self to contain her overwhelming affect. It was clearly inappropriate to offer Margaret art materials or expect her to engage in imaginative activity through the substance and body of the materials. The art materials would remain just that, simply materials with no latent possibility for development through symbolic use. There was a psyche/soma split being acted out by Margaret and I was feeling it too. My capacity for rational or *directed* thinking was impaired. My clever or 'artful' bits were rendered useless and there was no way I could think or theorise in this session – I could only feel.

My inner voice became quite critical and asked what I thought I was actually doing. This inner voice took on the persona of a good friend of mine who was, in reality, a very relaxed and adaptable mother, a vital care-giver and real go-getter in her ability to fend for her children as a lone parent. In my imagination I could hear her saying, 'So what are you doing then? What's art therapy all about? What do art therapists actually do?' The answer to this question appeared to be that nothing was being done. I simply didn't know what to do. I considered going and doing something useful with my time, reading what notes or case history might be available or talking to the staff on duty to try and find out if something had triggered Margaret's behaviour. I also felt tempted by the lure of becoming a real care-giver, offering a glass of water maybe or some other remedy for her distress. The temptation to become an actual mother rather than remain a symbolic one was strong.

I decided to remain with my confusion and was grateful for the shield Margaret's closed door afforded me. Sitting alone feeling rejected and de-skilled, my art materials redundant, my capacity for directed thinking lost to me, it was my own inner images or fantasies that gave a clue to the early infantile nature of Margaret's rage and her own persecutory inner voices. I later realised how important it was to stay with her distress and that, although I did not have some vital remedy for the situation, it was my actual bodily presence that might indicate to Margaret I could be relied upon to maintain a therapeutic space, an external equivalent of Margaret's absent inner psychic space. I subjectively experienced this absence as an attack on my ability to be an art therapist. My capacity to think had become impaired and split from the body or substance of the art materials, which at the time I thought objectively could not be nourishing and good; their symbolic potential was lost to me.

Clearly if I was going to find a way forward with Margaret and the split between subject and object was to be bridged through symbolic activity, the action and

80 Alison Goldsmith

experience of the sessions would need to happen not just in our inner worlds but in a shared space between us. It was to be the art materials that later enabled that process to occur when a few weeks later Margaret used her favourite colours to make an image called 'pink boat on blue sea' (Figure 6.2). It was different from her previous drawings, which depicted her external world, a world in which random objects and events appeared in an unconnected way. This image suggested

Figure 6.2 Pink boat on blue sea

a more integrated subjective experience of merger; the sea is all-encompassing and the small boat looks likely to be overwhelmed. It isn't entirely about subjectivity, however, because she had succeeded in using the art materials to represent an experience of being 'at sea'. The art materials and the image provided an interface between her inner and outer world, between cognition and emotion.

There were days when Margaret was asleep on her bed when I arrived and the staff on duty would be apologetic that they had not succeeded in rousing her. At such times I would enter her room, provided I was reasonably sure that I was not an unwelcome intrusive presence. I would make a verbal statement about the fact that I was there and that she was sleeping and would make a drawing of her asleep with her teddy. I remained in her room for the duration of the session. I would date the drawing and leave it with a written message that I would be back the following week. Hopefully Margaret would understand that I had been there for her although she appeared to be absent. These early sessions, with my client asleep and me, the therapist, doing the drawing, might have looked like failures to the casual observer. Surprisingly I didn't feel too uncomfortable about them. I appreciated the time and space afforded by the session and my thinking about Margaret was enhanced and facilitated through my own reverie in making the drawing. There were no critical inner voices and I did not feel self-conscious about the apparent lack of engagement between Margaret and myself.

As I sat drawing Margaret asleep with her teddy there were once again obvious associations with early infancy. In those silent sessions two people from very different and opposing theoretical backgrounds came to mind as an unlikely but helpful couple; one was Uta Frith, who I recalled had made the point that autism was not only associated with childhood but also with development and adulthood: 'Autism starts to be noticed in childhood, but it is not a disorder of childhood. Instead it is a disorder of development' (Frith, 1999). The other was Michael Fordham, whose work with children was the foundation of the developmental school of analytical psychology.

Fordham was a Jungian analyst who worked with autistic children and his experience with them caused him to question Jung's concept of individuation, a concept Jung thought only possible after ego development had facilitated adaptation to the environment (1921: para. 760). Fordham postulated the idea of a primary self, suggesting the infant begins life as an integrated person separate from the mother and comes into relation with her through a process of de-integration. This is a process in which the infant makes an active contribution to the mother/infant interaction (Fordham, 1985). He saw the infant's life as a repeating pattern of de-integration, observable through the process of feeding (and I would add reverie and play to this) and integration, as in sleep. 'De-integration and integration describe a fluctuating state of learning in which the infant opens itself to new experiences and then withdraws in order to reintegrate and consolidate those experiences' (Fordham, 1989: 64). Fordham's theory recognises the importance of the infant/mother interaction but I think it also allows for the possibility that the success of that relationship does not rest solely with the mother but also with the infant. Fordham saw this fluctuating process as releasing a capacity for adaptation that is not a mechanical acquiescence to environmental realities, not the kind of adaptation associated with the ego and often seen in the rather rigid traits of autistic people, but an active, positive process of 'bringing influence to bear on reality and mastering it as part of a struggle for existence' (Fordham, 1989: 52). The primary process of adaptation, if it follows a normal course of development, is a healthy struggle that results in the subject meeting the outside world and making some impression on it in a relationship of give and take. The pathological equivalent of this process, as in autism, results in early defences of the self being constelled or fixed.

Fordham endorsed attempts to bring psychological theories of the development of the self in line with biological ones by acknowledging that the infant is born with capacities for adaptation. However, his concept of a developmental process differs from that of the biologists and ethologists in that it is not only a *physiological* process but a *psychic* one with an outer process of interaction between mother and infant and a corresponding inner process between psyche and soma (Fordham, 1989).

Margaret was certainly 'bringing influence to bear on reality' in the context of coming into relation with me. In the light of Fordham's theory her need to sleep through her art therapy session may be seen in a more positive way. My subjective experience of these sessions was certainly positive: I was able to consolidate and integrate what I, like Margaret, had experienced as being overwhelming in our meetings. I was also able to give something of myself to Margaret in the drawings I left for her.

In the early days of the work there were often times when I was obliged to sit it out with her in this way. However, the frequency of these occasions diminished. Whereas she would once remain in her room on 'bad' days, she began to come downstairs more frequently and we would manage the bad days together.

When she was able to leave the confines of her own room we met in the kitchen. It was large, light and airy, had a spacious table on which to spread materials and a water supply. It was possible to close the door and establish a secure space in which to meet usually, though not always, undisturbed and free from interruption. In fact most of these advantages went unused because Margaret chose to sit in an armchair wedged tightly into a corner of the room. I was obliged to sit in a cramped position and had to bring in a small table inferior to the one already in the kitchen and she would work from the safety of her armchair. Attempts on my part to introduce paints were unsuccessful as she always chose to use crayons. Sometimes these meetings, sitting as she was with her back to the wall, had a more defensive and stuck quality to them than the times when she was either sleeping or too disturbed to contemplate using art materials. Although the sessions in the kitchen were manageable, in the sense that Margaret had more composure and produced more images, I always felt that the real work was done in the more disturbed sessions. I had experienced these early turbulent sessions as having more movement and possibility for change or re-constellation. In retrospect, what might have looked like failures at the time were in fact the foundations of our work together.

Two of Margaret's symptoms I referred to earlier, her 'voices' and rigid repetitive games of I-spy, were a predominant feature in our face-to-face meetings. It seemed that the overwhelming affect she sometimes experienced and projected into me was at other times personified in her voices; her affect took shape or became objectified. This was evident in her image-making when the voices were represented by a pink shape, resembling the dresses she had often previously drawn and she drew herself with a white crayon on white paper underneath the voices, inconspicuous and barely visible in relation to them.

In another session Margaret drew two figures on separate sheets of paper (Figure 6.3). One depicted an 'angry voice' and was drawn using a bright yellow crayon. The figure had a large 'v' above it and Margaret had not previously used yellow. The other figure was in a softer colour, ochre, and was a portrait of me with an accurate tonal representation of the colours I was wearing at the time. Margaret's choice of colour to portray me is softer than the brighter, more intense yellow of the voices. However, I do think this portrayal of me has an association with the angry voice and says something about the difficulty of being in the presence of someone else in a reciprocal relationship, involving give and take. Margaret's voices may have been a way of managing the painful and difficult moments she experienced when her inner life threatened to spill over and spoil her art therapy session and possibly damage me.

The inner persecutory voices that in the previous more disturbed sessions I had 'heard' or imagined in my mind, I now experienced with affective intensity. On

Figure 6.3 Two separate figures

reflection, however, I was able to say it was *as if* my ego and capacity to function were lost to me along with the art materials. Margaret may have been some way from having an *as if* relationship to her voices but it was a beginning and her voices were a way of giving shape and meaning to her affect, thus owning rather than projecting it.

Margaret's choice of materials was very limited. Apart from the one session when she used the yellow crayons, she chose almost exclusively to use pink or blue. I tried to strike a balance between meeting her needs and not colluding or acquiescing. I provided her with a box of materials consisting predominantly of the kind of colours and crayons that she liked to use. These were kept in her room between sessions, and were identifiable as hers and belonged with her in the home. I brought with me every week my case in which I had my own materials and often there were things in there that I had been using with another client on the previous day. Our two sets of materials, hers and mine, would on 'good' days, be permitted to co-exist and mingle on the rather fragile table between us.

One piece of material Margaret chose was some red cellophane, which I had introduced rather playfully one day when I myself was feeling clumsy and intrusive. I held it to my eyes and looked at Margaret through it using it as a kind of filter and sharing with her the warmth of the colour. Seeing and looking at her directly I felt might invoke a sense of shame in which the voices were more likely to be constellated, as hinted in the previous session when she drew the two yellow figures. It seemed important to find a way of acknowledging the shame of her being the sole object of my attention. The cellophane provided an alternative to a verbal interpretation that may have been too intrusive. The red material was initially a shield for us both, mediating the painful intensity of seeing and being seen. However, it soon became a playful way of seeing things differently, particularly when used in the game of I-spy. It was no longer just a barrier, although it was sometimes used in this way, as when the window cleaner suddenly appeared at the window one day. It was also taken on trips to the park or shops when Margaret went out with another therapist or her care assistant. It really became a symbolic object in the truest sense that it had more than one meaning. It mediated between us both and between Margaret and her experience of the outside world, although it was also sometimes used as a defensive, autistic object.

Over a period of time the game of I-spy also became more alive and animated, with real feelings being experienced and communicated. What had once felt like a rigid structure became a safe structure, an ordered pattern or game plan in which the spontaneity and relinquishing of control needed for reciprocity was allowed to happen. The game took a similar route to her image-making process. Margaret was able to progress from spying/describing disembodied objects such as 'D for dress' to feeling-toned words: 'F for feelings'; 'A for adorable', 'something I was when I was little'; 'E for escape'; 'S for state', 'something I get in sometimes'.

It was in a game of I-spy that Margaret allowed herself to experience a profound sense of loss. 'L for life' opened up a string of word associations communicating the fact that her mother's partner of many years had died and Margaret had not gone home that weekend as a result. I later had it confirmed that this was an actual event, not a fantasy of Margaret's, although I had not been informed about this and the staff on duty that day did not know. During this labyrinthine and emotional game of I-spy, Margaret asked me if I had a nice life. This was no envious attack on me, as in the early violent sessions, but an imaginative act of reparation and coming to terms with loss.

Margaret's self-images became more embodied as our work together progressed and there was often uncertainty rather than confusion in her interpretation of who was who and whether one or both of the figures represented her; the theme of two figures on one sheet of paper continued and the figures were usually touching. I prepared Margaret for the closure of our work together well in advance of the final session and her touching figures gradually became separated until by the final session the two figures were actually on separate pages.

In an account of his work in an analytic setting, Ian Alister describes how he managed to overcome a stalemate with a patient who had no spontaneity, an internal silent world and no dreams that could be shared. He discovered, quite by chance, that he and his patient shared an interest in football. This interactive game provided a metaphor, a third area in the analytic setting in which play could begin between him and his patient.

> The process of playing is much more than establishing a rapport; it may at times constitute the very conditions of existence. Sport offers a mode of interaction that by-passes defences which continually frustrate a more 'meaningful' exchange. The meaning is in the feeling rather than the thinking, and the feeling is generated in the reciprocity of the exchange. Establishing the to and fro is vital.
>
> (Alister, 1998: 234)

Afterword

My chapter began life as an essay, 'A critical evaluation of applying concepts derived from analytical psychology to therapeutic work with an autistic adult', which was part of a taught MA in Jung and Post-Jungian Studies. The original essay was born out of necessity; I was required to appraise the applicability of Jungian modes of enquiry to a chosen topic for which I had some investment and knowledge. I was working with Margaret at the time and the practical realities of the work seemed irreconcilable with the theoretical headiness of academia. I looked at areas of research into autism, most notably Central Coherence Theory (Frith, 1999), and it became apparent that what cognitive science had identified as impaired or absent in autistic people, 'an ability to draw together diverse information to construct higher-level meaning in context' (Happé, 1999: 116) was a central tenet of Jungian psychology. With hindsight I can see this is descriptive of a central concept in analytical psychology, that of the *complexes* and the *ego complex* in particular.

A complex is a conflict in the psyche that is marked by affect and can become manifest when associative material is expressed in the form of images and ideas. Complexes provide the connecting principle between the collective (archetypal) and the personal and the role of imagination is vital to this process; 'without such a concept it would be difficult to express just how experience is built up; psychological life would be a series of unconnected incidents' (Samuels *et al.*, 1991: 34). I acknowledge the apparent incompatibility between Jungian concepts and autistic impairments at the beginning of my chapter, but I think my dilemma is more vividly encapsulated in the image of me 'offering a starving refugee art materials'. It's easy, with hindsight, to see my own *ego-complex* constellated when I felt de-skilled and my clever and artful 'bits' were rendered useless and remained *unconnected* from the therapeutic process.

I find it interesting that it is one of Jung's earliest concepts that orientates me when thinking again about how I was cut adrift in the challenging context of autism. Jung was developing his 'complex' theory as early as 1904 during his time of collaboration with Freud and it preceded his ideas on *archetypes* and *active imagination*. Jung's 'complexes' have their roots in dissociation and grew out of his work on word association tests, which he considered gave empirical evidence of the autonomous existence of the unconscious.

Some readers might think I was using active imagination to guide me in my work with Margaret, but I think my 'inner' images had a more spontaneous quality to them and were not the result of active imagination, which requires the subject to 'concentrate on a specific point, mood, picture or event which allow a chain of associated Fantasies to develop' (Samuels *et al.*, 1991: 9). This describes a more conscious process, whereas I think I was guided by my unconscious processes.

In the intervening years I have trained as a psychoanalytic psychotherapist in a pluralist tradition and have often thought about my earlier work with Margaret in the context of other psychodynamic theories. Lacan's *mirror stage*, for example, describes the formation of the ego as arising from the infant's primary identification with her own *specular* image. The infant's visual perception develops in advance of her bodily coordination; she sees her own mirror image as a whole (a Gestalt) but this can be problematic in synthesis with her bodily self, which is uncoordinated at this stage and may be experienced, by comparison, as a *fragmented body*. This disparity, and the attendant anxiety, is resolved when the infant identifies with the wholeness of her mirror image; the identification gives her an *imaginary* sense of mastery over her muscular coordination which she has not yet actually achieved (Lacan, 1951 in Evans, 2005: 115).

For Lacan, the *mirror stage* 'marks a decisive turning point in the mental development of the child' (Lacan, 1951 in Evans, 2005: 115) and moreover one that requires an act of imagination or, in Lacanian terms, an introduction into the *imaginary order*. It's not difficult to see how a deficit in the development of imagination might result in leaving the infant with a fragmented sense of self.

In more recent years the work of Jean Knox, a Jungian analyst, combines Jung's concept of *archetypes* with attachment theory to explore how mind and meaning emerge through a developmental process and experience of interpersonal relationships. She outlines the similarities between Jung's concept of the complex and the 'internal working model' of attachment theory and acknowledges the role of the complex as a defence against unbearable experiences (Knox, 2003: 89–102). She doesn't write about autism; in fact, when writing on the *reflective function,* she is careful to make a distinction between the failure of the reflective function as a developmental deficit (as in autism) and the avoidance of it as an unconscious defence (Knox, 2003: 145). However, she says, 'The imaginative world, in all its richness, is the thread that links psyche and soma and that weaves archetypes, attachment and analysis together into a synthesis of the developmental, emergent and introjective aspects of the human mind' (Knox, 2003: 207).

There will always be a favoured, prevailing theory both in the wider field of research and also for each of us as individual therapists in our own clinical practice. Jung suggests that the personality of the therapist is 'the great healing factor' (Jung, 1958: para. 198) and cautions against seeking agreement on different theories which can only result in one-sidedness and dessication: 'many theories are needed before we can get even a rough picture of the psyche's complexity' (Jung, 1958: para. 198). Had I written this chapter in more recent years it would almost certainly be informed by different theories; I hope this reflects an ongoing process in my professional development rather than abandoning one theory in favour of another. We may look at the same subject from a different viewpoint, but it is the *way* we look at it and our own individual subjectivity that is central to the effective integration of theory into practice.

References

Alister, I. (1998) 'Popular culture: keeping ourselves together', in Alister, I. and Hauke, C. (eds), *Contemporary Jungian Analysis*, London: Routledge.
Evans, D. (2005) *An Introductory Dictionary of Lacanian Analysis*, London: Routledge.
Fordham, M. (1976) *The Self and Autism*, London: Heinemann.
—— (1985) 'Integration–deintegration in infancy', *Explorations into the Self: The Library of Analytical Psychology*, London: Academic Press.
—— (1989) 'The infant's reach: reflections on maturation in early life', *Psychological Perspectives*, 21: 59–76.
Frith, U. (1999) *Autism Explaining the Enigma*, Oxford: Blackwell.
Halliday, D. (1978) 'The use of therapeutic art in child guidance' in Elliot, D. (ed.), *The Inner Eye,* Oxford: Catalogue Museum of Modern Art.
Happé, F. (1999) *Autism: An Introduction to Psychological Theory*, Hove: Psychology Press.
Jung, C.G. (1917) 'The synthetic or constructive method', *Collected Works 7*, London: Routledge.
—— (1921) 'Definitions', *Collected Works 6*, London: Routledge.
—— (1956) 'Two kinds of thinking', *Collected Works 5*, London: Routledge.
—— (1958) 'Medicine and psychotherapy', *Collected Works 16*, London: Routledge.
—— (1960) 'The transcendent function', *Collected Works 8*, London: Routledge.

Knox, J. (2003) *Archetype, Attachment, Analysis: Jungian Psychology and the Emergent Mind*, London: Brunner-Routledge.
Samuels, A., Shorter, B. and Plaut, F. (1991) *A Critical Dictionary of Jungian Analysis*, London: Routledge.
Schaverien, J. (1992) *The Revealing Image*, London: Tavistock/Routledge.

Chapter 7

A collaborative art therapy approach

Elizabeth Ashby

Introduction

This chapter explores the development of a collaborative approach to art therapy with a severely learning disabled client, whose behaviour was challenging and consistent with the autistic spectrum. The rationale for this approach is presented and illustrated with a case study conducted in two phases. The first phase consisted of individual sessions with me over two years and the second phase was a further two years of collaborative sessions with myself and a music therapist. This proved to be an effective therapeutic model that resulted in greater impulse control for the client and the development of his intersubjective interactions. Additionally, it enabled us to develop our practice and expand our individual expertise and creativity. The collaboration deepened the therapeutic relationship, facilitated movement in the therapy when it felt stuck, and reduced the emotional impact of the work on the therapists.

The setting

I worked for a number of years alongside a music therapist, a drama therapist, a speech and language therapist and a team of care staff in a specialist day unit for people with severe learning disabilities and challenging behaviour. 'Gentle teaching' (McGee *et al.*, 1987) was used in the centre, an approach that seeks to understand challenging behaviour, including violence (physical and verbal), self-injurious and withdrawing behaviours, and offer alternative ways of managing it that do not involve restraint if possible. 'Intensive interaction' (Hewett *et al.*, 2011) was also introduced, focusing on pre-verbal communication with autistic clients. Both of these approaches were congruent with our intersubjective, client-centred approach to therapy.

Our clients had restricted or no speech, suffered from physical difficulties such as epilepsy and displayed aspects of autistic spectrum disorders. They were difficult to work with therapeutically because they found it hard to process thoughts, communicate and establish relationships. We were always on our guard as their behaviour was often violent and destructive. Sensitivity to their communication was essential: we had to be aware of mood, body language, vocalisations, and unravel confusing qualities of their speech. Therapeutic relationships took a long time to establish and we used all the resources available to us, particularly our personal qualities of patience and tenacity.

The difficulties we experienced working with this client group were considerable and challenged all we had learnt in our training. The basic tenets we took for granted in therapy – the sort of space we could use, the expectation we could speak about issues and personal safety – were not usually available to us. Many of our clients had difficulty staying in a room for any length of time and were unable to tell us what they were thinking or feeling. Their use of materials was usually at the pre-representational stage, and knowing them well was no guarantee they would not hit you.

Furthermore, the building we worked in was overcrowded, chaotic and noisy, and consequently was not particularly conducive to therapy. A high turnover of staff, lack of understanding of our roles among the day unit staff and inconsistent management of the centre compounded many of the problems we faced.

As a therapy team we worked well together and supported one another. By combining our expertise and our thinking we developed the therapeutic work and helped each other to cope with countertransference feelings of being drained, exhausted and 'wiped out' as a result of the slow pace of therapy. The development of our collaborative work took place over time, and we all had to manage feelings of frustration, of being stuck periodically, of being de-skilled and unable to think.

Colin

Colin was 19 when I first started working with him and was a tall, well-built, active and excitable young man. He needed a full timetable that kept his interest but also needed containment. He became agitated in noisy, crowded places but play was important to him and he enjoyed art. He had limited speech, communicating in the third person in short sentences, with a restricted range of vocabulary. It was not safe for him to be alone for any period of time because he was unpredictable and would hit people if they annoyed him, and he would get into areas that were unsafe. When excited his behaviour became increasingly challenging and could become dangerous towards those around him, so the staff tried to reduce stimulation and his anticipation of upcoming events. He had little understanding of personal boundaries and had difficulty separating feelings of affection from his developing sexuality. Colin had experienced disruption and neglect in early childhood, before his carer became involved in his life. These deprivations, combined with his severe learning disability and autistic traits, made relationships hard for him to understand.

Colin was referred for art therapy because he loved drawing and because the day staff working with him found it hard to balance his need to be fully and actively occupied with his inability to wait for anything. They found him difficult to communicate with, and prone to violence when frustrated or upset. The staff and I talked to him about starting 'art therapy sessions' but he probably understood little more than that it involved 'colouring'.

Colin's first individual session

Colin just arrived at the art room door without me having to go and get him, greeted me enthusiastically, saying 'Hello Li[z]', and went straight to the art room cupboard and started getting materials out. He knew what he wanted and chose chunky crayons, chalks, pencils and felt tips, lots of stencils and shapes, and a handful of sheets of paper. I asked him to choose just one sheet of paper to work on, and after a bit of negotiation we compromised on two, while he put the other sheets to one side.

He drew round some shapes in different colours using pencils, markers and a biro and then did a big scrawl over the paper with a crayon, repeating the process on the other side (Figure 7.1). He did four pictures in this way. The first two pictures he put in his bag saying they were for his carer and I did not stop him because I knew this was what he usually did when he did 'colouring'. We negotiated that he would also leave two in the room with me.

Every now and then he said 'Look' after he'd drawn something. I tried to show my attentiveness by saying 'It's a circle' or 'It's blue and orange'. In one of his pictures he drew round his hand many times, and looked for my approval. He made no comment in response to my remarks about his pictures and there was little engagement with me except when he said 'Look' and when he touched me. Once he took my hand and pressed the palm to his lips very gently, and several

Figure 7.1 Circles

times he pulled my head towards him and put his mouth to the top of it, also very gently. He was extremely restrained, and appeared to be on his best behaviour. He stayed for forty minutes and then abruptly got up to leave, saying 'Finish'. I asked him to help me clear up, which he did rather carelessly and then rushed away with his pictures. Colin seemed to have discharged some tension through his image-making and the very restrained manner of his behaviour suggested an awareness of something new happening.

First phase of therapy

Colin was restrained during the early sessions but after a few weeks his behaviour became more challenging. He demonstrated an affection for me that seemed to reflect his confusion about appropriate personal boundaries and made him jealous of other people's contact with me outside the sessions. Boundary issues were central to our work both in helping Colin to understand my role and the need to stay in the room for the session. I worked at keeping his contact with me as non-intrusive and non-sexual as possible, keeping to the time boundaries of the session, and preventing intrusions from others.

Sessions generally lasted 45 minutes, during which Colin concentrated hard on his image-making. At the beginning of our work he would take many sheets of paper from the cupboard, handfuls of pens, pencils, stencils and other materials, working through several sheets of paper, pressing hard on the pens and destroying the nibs, breaking pencil leads, and making holes in the paper. He drew chaotic spirals and circles, channelling his aggression and excitement into his image-making, working rapidly on both sides of the paper.

After about fifteen minutes Colin became calmer in the session and his work became gentler and more purposeful. He liked to use stencils to draw round, sometimes naming them, and often he would draw round one of his hands or mine, asking me for help when he felt he needed it (Figure 7.2). He often used the same phrase to mean several different things, for instance 'Help draw it' might mean he wanted me to do part of the drawing or he wanted me to hold the stencil down, he wanted me to do it for him or he wanted me to watch him do it. The particular meaning became evident through trial and error.

Although I wished to give Colin as much freedom and choice as possible, I also had to restrict some of his activities to prevent them becoming dangerous, while providing containment and positive reinforcement. Restrictions were necessary largely as a result of difficulties with communication. Only by showing Colin what I meant could I introduce a way of being in the therapeutic space to him. Containing the mess and chaos of the session was difficult because if I imposed the boundaries too rigidly there was always the risk that he would spiral into aggression. I started to limit how much paper he got out of the cupboard, put aside his own supply of pens and pencils to prevent him destroying all the materials, and built up a collection of different stencils he could use, introducing new shapes such as animals, numbers, letters, vehicles, people and shops.

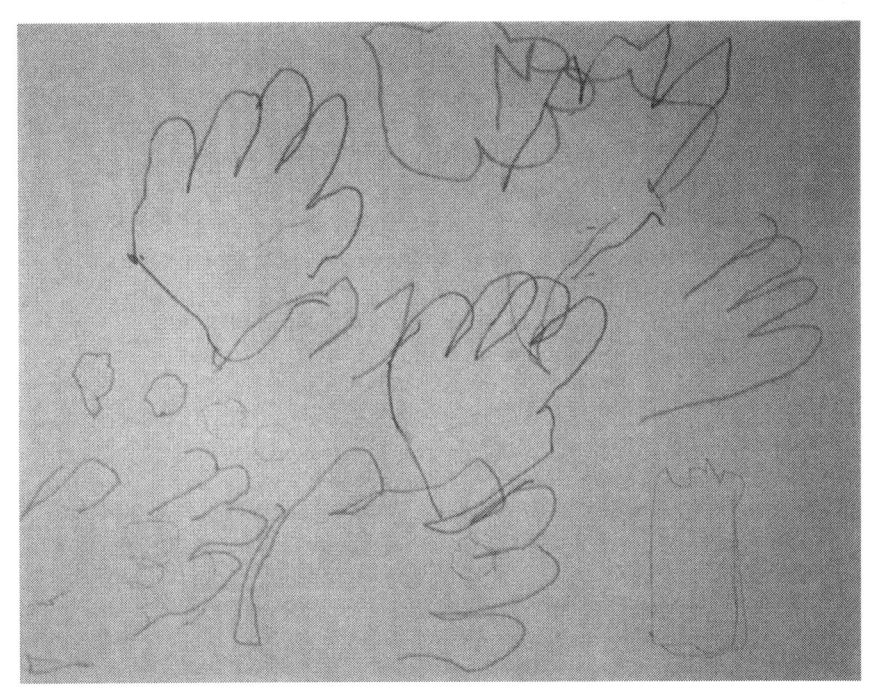

Figure 7.2 Hands

Keeping the images in the room was another issue, as he wanted to take them all with him. We compromised and he would take one or two. He would put them in his home bag for his carer, and they served as an aid to communication between them about the events of his day.

Time boundaries were not easy to keep either. Colin never wanted to wait for anything so having to wait for his session was very difficult for him. He banged on the door while I got the room ready, or on the windows from the outside, and I felt as if I was under siege. It took approximately eighteen months before he finally accepted he had to wait for his session, and the first time he waited patiently in the lobby felt like a major achievement.

Colin related to me with a mixture of affection and aggression. He would try to hug and kiss me, which I resisted but could not entirely prevent, sometimes feeling positively molested by him, while at other times he could be gentle and appropriate. I had to be careful where I sat because he would put his arm round my neck, pull me towards him and kiss the top of my head or sink his teeth lightly into my skull. I discouraged this and after a time a strategy was developed in the centre to try and encourage Colin to shake hands with people instead of more intrusive behaviour. I also found it was wise not to wear earrings and to keep my hair tied back.

Communication was difficult and affected the countertransference considerably. Colin communicated in short sentences in the third person. 'Hello, Li[z]' he would say to me, 'Look' (pointing to his picture, taking my hand and putting it on it). Sometimes he looked at me, giggling, and waving his arms excitedly, and saying a few words about something on his mind such as 'Colin go walk'. The hardest part of the sessions for me was long periods when he was drawing and would not speak at all; he would frequently ignore me when I spoke to him, going into a sort of trance. This process has been described by Stack (1998) and Rostron (2010) as the client moving in and out of his encapsulated shell. During these periods I gradually felt increasingly exhausted and struggled to stay attentive, even awake. This countertransference sometimes felt unbearable, and I felt 'wiped out' and annihilated by it. It was hard to think about the cause of these feelings. On reflection I identified frustration as a result of the very slow pace of the therapy, and I wonder if they were also a response to an unconscious communication by Colin of his own unbearable and overwhelming feelings.

As time went on I found the slow pace more and more frustrating in my work with him. I thought there was probably still much that could be done with Colin in therapy, for instance working on relationship issues such as sharing. However, I felt worn down and drained by the countertransference, the effort of maintaining the boundaries, the repetitive nature of the images and their method of production, and the painfully slow rate of progress. After two years of sessions I thought a change was needed to breathe new life into the work.

Collaborative sessions

As a team we discussed the possibility of either the music therapist or the drama therapist joining me, and what form the sessions might take. We had begun to experiment with new combinations and approaches, and in Colin's case we decided that we would see what happened if the music therapist joined me and worked with the art materials too. Colin already knew Mark, the music therapist, which felt advantageous. I took the lead in sessions while he supported my work as appropriate. Both of us had a client-centred and non-directive approach, and in my work with Colin I had brought as much of this model of therapy as I could. Mark and I talked to Colin about Mark joining our sessions, and Colin seemed willing for this to happen.

For the first joint session Colin and I carried on our session much the same as usual, except that Mark was in the room too. We just tried it out to see what would happen, being prepared to adjust our approach until we had a sense of whether it was working or not.

We were not sure if Colin would accept Mark's presence in the session, but he seemed happy he was there. It had become customary for me to walk down the corridor to the lobby area and invite Colin to his session and on this occasion we both did so. He came quite happily, although he seemed more excited than usual. The furniture was arranged with two tables pushed against the wall and the materials set aside for Colin in the centre. Colin sat in the middle with me on one side as we usually did, so Mark sat on the other side.

Figure 7.3 Animals, shapes and colours

Colin said 'Hello' to both of us, giggled, waved his arms in front of him, and then selected a handful of felt pens and a sheet of paper. He started to draw spiralling circles very hard and fast on the paper, making holes in it because he pressed so hard, and then he turned it over and began to do the same on the other side (Figure 7.3). When he felt the drawing was finished he shoved it to one side and took another sheet from the pile and began to draw round his hand. He asked us both to 'Look', which we did enthusiastically.

As Colin was drawing, Mark took a piece of paper, a pencil and a stencil and began to draw, but Colin stopped me from drawing, as he usually did. He seemed quite excited, was less in control of his actions and quite rough with me, pulling me about quite a lot, trying to kiss the top of my head and pull me towards him. Mark became concerned and suggested to Colin that he and I swapped seats, which Colin did not object to, and consequently I was less vulnerable.

Colin became calmer as the session went on, and after making two very quick images messily and somewhat frantically, he settled down to drawing more carefully, enlisting help from both of us to draw round several stencils. I had introduced some jumbo sized pencils and some vehicle stencils to the supply of materials kept solely for his use, and he was very pleased with them. Mark drew a deer, grass and sky, and tried to talk to Colin about his drawing, but got little response. Colin stayed for the whole of his session time, and then said 'Finish' and got up to leave the room. He left us one of the more frantically drawn pictures.

We reflected on the session and felt that on the whole it had been a success. We were surprised and pleased at how easily Colin had accepted Mark's presence in the session, but we felt adjustments needed to be made, particularly with regard to the arrangement of the furniture. We re-arranged it so that Mark sat nearest the door, and I had more space from Colin so he could not reach me so easily; also we could move away from Colin and put the table between us if he became too aggressive.

Mark was enthusiastic as he gave me feedback about his observations, pointing out that quite a change had taken place in Colin during his period of individual art therapy sessions with me, which I had found hard to perceive due to the slow pace, small incremental steps of change and my proximity to the situation. Mark found Colin more tolerant, more able to share, and that he demonstrated a greater degree of concentration. He appeared to have slowed down considerably, was more able to wait for his session and was less aggressive. This feedback was very encouraging.

After a few weeks Colin began to test the relationships by interacting with one of us during the session and ignoring the other, until after a few weeks he managed to relate to both of us most of the time. He allowed Mark to draw but would not tolerate me drawing. He related to me in the same manner as he had previously but was concerned about sharing me with Mark. He sparred with him for a few weeks, and we were aware of the risk factor it represented. Later we realised that Colin had allowed Mark to become an active role model figure who used the materials as he did, in a similar fashion to a son relating to a father and imitating his actions. However, he needed me to remain fully attentive. The dynamics of a parental dyad had begun to emerge and oedipal issues of rivalry, envy and desire were evident.

We worked hard on the issue of sharing. Colin did not want to share me, or the materials. He would push his paper onto Mark's, limiting his space, and slap him if he took a pen. Mark said, 'That's not very nice. How can I draw now?' and moved the paper up. Then Mark might say 'Please can I have the blue pen, Colin?' and Colin might throw one at him. After a while he learned to share the space on the table and the materials but if he was in an aggressive mood the tension would be tangible. At such times we would sit quietly, not speaking, hardly moving, attempting to reduce and contain the tension, aware of the risk of an incident. Usually the tension would dispel after Colin had channelled some of his aggressive feelings into the art work, to our considerable relief.

We decided to use Mark's production of images as a means of modelling development for Colin. Mark would imitate some of Colin's methods, such as using a stencil to draw round, or drawing round his hand, and then would develop that into a whole picture. If Mark had drawn an animal we would name it, put it in a landscape, imitate the sounds it might make, and encourage Colin to join in a dialogue about the image. We made exaggerated responses to situations, perhaps feigning distress if he did something we did not like, and he gradually became more sensitive to our needs. This approach could be seen to be a variation of the 'interactive square' described by Bragge and Fenner (2009).

After six months of collaborative therapy sessions we noticed a difference in his verbal communication. At first Colin ignored both of us for periods of time, and communicated in a limited manner. Then he initiated verbal interaction with us more frequently, on more diverse topics, and an element of play developed which Colin really enjoyed. Sometimes we all laughed together. Thus Colin's verbal development seemed to be taking the course that a small child's does as he interacts with his parents.

There was an aspect to his image-making that had been quite rigid but began to change over time. A few weeks after our joint sessions started he began to copy Mark's actions, such as when he drew a shape. We encouraged him to make shapes more solid by colouring them in rather than only drawing their outlines, with Mark demonstrating, and to draw freely without stencils; our hope was to foster the development of representational skills and spontaneity.

However, Mark and I both found that a sense of weariness overcame us like a numbing blanket. Colin would ignore one or both of us for long periods while he concentrated on drawing, seeming to go into a sort of spaced-out trance that made us feel tired and drained. Often, as a result of the continual repetitions in his art work and interactions, we felt bored. We felt pressure to act out our feelings and 'switch off' and we had to work hard to stay attentive, talking about Mark's and Colin's image-making to resist the pressure, and addressing it in supervision.

It was always hard work to contain the mess Colin made. We consistently reinforced the boundaries about how much paper and how many pens he could use – one at a time instead of handfuls – and the pen lids would be everywhere. He was still not very tolerant of clearing up. Gradually he became more receptive and compliant, but if he was in an aggressive mood it was still a risk.

Figure 7.4 Rabbits

After a year working collaboratively a sense of design began to be apparent in Colin's images. He drew round a motorbike stencil and created a whole line of them; then he drew lines of other shapes such as rabbits (Figure 7.4). Another time he drew shapes all round the edge of the paper, and began to do this with lots of different images, for instance putting a rabbit in each corner of the paper and one in the middle, demonstrating greater spatial awareness. He began to interact with Mark by turn-taking – Mark would draw something and then hand Colin the pen, and Colin would draw something. He would occasionally watch Mark and copy what he was doing. This simple act seemed like a milestone to us, and suggested Colin was developing a capacity for reflection, unlike his earlier sessions which were characterised by his consuming the materials.

Towards an ending

Another six months passed and Colin's medication was changed due to fears about the long-term effects of one he had been on for several years. Colin began to leave his session early and for a few weeks he only managed to stay for about 15 minutes.

Gradually his sessions resumed their normal length, and then another medication change took place and he began to demand art materials first thing in the morning when he arrived and at other times. I encouraged the staff to make a range of art materials available to him, and space in the art room when possible. It became clear that as a result of our therapeutic work Colin had learned to channel his aggressive feelings into his image-making and now asked for art materials himself when he felt he needed to draw to reduce his tension, and as a result his need for therapy sessions came to a natural end. We had worked collaboratively with him for two years, bringing the total amount of therapy time to four years.

Therapeutic gains

The therapeutic gains from the first individual phase of art therapy were encouraging once Mark helped me to recognise them. Progress was so slow that I might have ended my input there, except that I still thought there was much that could be achieved by continuing my work with Colin if I could find a suitable approach. It is poignant to recognise that severely learning disabled clients experience much loss in their lives on many different levels, particularly in terms of relationships with staff who become important to them but who often do not stay for very long.

The collaborative phase of therapy proved to be successful in consolidating the early one-to-one work. Joint sessions provided containment and allowed different dynamics to emerge. As female and male co-therapists, I wondered if we represented traditional parental roles, although Colin apparently had not experienced this in early childhood until his current carer became involved in his life. Between us we had been able to contain and defuse tensions in the sessions.

Communication was enhanced, and Colin's linguistic ability and interaction increased noticeably, as did his verbal and pictorial communication. Colin demonstrated that he could manage his feelings better and had a greater ability to delay gratification.

Image-making was the main focus of our sessions, within which many relationship issues were worked out. Mark had to learn to develop visual media skills but always willingly drew on my expertise, and we found the collaboration very valuable. The effect of combining our knowledge was synergistic and significantly increased the creativity we were able to bring to sessions, as well as increasing our safety, our thinking capacity, and the therapeutic progress made. We also helped each other to weather the negative countertransference better than we could have done alone.

Art therapists and this client group

Tipple (1992) discusses the constraints of working with members of this client group, in terms of difficulties in establishing relationships, the repetitions in the art work and their quality, difficulties in understanding how the client is thinking and feeling, and managing challenging behaviour. Art therapists can feel de-skilled and disempowered in work with severely learning disabled individuals and the slow rate of change can lead to a feeling of hopelessness (Rabiger, 1998). Stack also discussed difficult feelings, describing her 'countertransference feelings of dizziness, headache and an inability to think' (1998: 106) and her difficulties when she 'became caught up in the resistance and frustration of extended periods of inertia' (1998: 108).

Fox (1998) suggests that art therapy sessions can facilitate some renegotiation of early developmental stages, providing the client receives adequate support from their therapist:

> Within an art therapy session, the client is provided with a regular boundaried time which has the quality of being more unstructured. It is structured by the therapist on the edge of a client's needs, so that there is always potentially a little more space to explore ... essentially Winnicott's 'potential space' ...
> (Fox, 1998: 77)

Parental dyad

Colin had a chronological age of 21 when we started collaborative sessions but a developmental age of about three years. It became apparent as sessions progressed that Colin had given us parental roles. Mark was to be the proactive member of the dyad who modelled different approaches to situations, as a father does with his child. In contrast, I was to remain passive and attentive to him throughout the session in a more stereotypically motherly role. He would not tolerate me using the art materials, growing angry if my attention was drawn away from him.

Colin's increasing awareness of this dynamic seemed to be very helpful to him. Colin is thought to have experienced a very chaotic, disturbed and fragmented childhood, characterised by negative attention from his birth mother who was not able to care for him adequately. Consequently, Colin had grown into a young man who often sought negative attention in a manner that could be violent and unmanageable. I felt he needed to be confident of my constant attention and availability, my 'gaze' upon him and his art work, to be able to take a maturational step forward, a process that Winnicott (1971) writes about in terms of the baby who sees him or herself reflected in the mother's face as he looks at her. From the available history, it seems likely that Colin did not have an adequate experience of the mirroring that a mother ordinarily provides for her child, and Winnicott suggests that there are negative consequences for the baby who does not see himself reflected in his mother's face, including that their creativity tends to atrophy. Colin's learning disability and autistic traits probably also impacted upon his capacity to respond to his mother. Co-therapists can reflect aspects of early relationships with primary caregivers that many clients have lacked, and model ways of relating that are helpful to autistic clients who find relationships difficult to understand.

Winnicott (1971: 63) says that the work takes place within 'the overlap of the two play areas, that of the patient and that of the therapist'. In my individual sessions with Colin there was some evidence of this, but there was much greater development of the overlap of play within the art work in the collaborative sessions. I believe this gave rise to Colin's ability to be more creative and to incorporate more spontaneous design into his imagery.

Collaborative work

The most established co-therapy model within the profession is that of an experienced art therapist and a trainee co-facilitating an art therapy group, such as the one described by Fox (1998). In her example, the group of autistic clients seemed busy and potentially chaotic, but benefited from the containment (both practical and psychological) that two therapists were able to offer. This reinforced Fox's ability to be objective, and was 'like a family situation with young children, having two "parents"' (Fox, 1998: 81).

In my research survey (Ashby 2004, 2011), I found that art therapists who work collaboratively mostly do so with groups, although some work collaboratively with individual clients. Many art therapists collaborate with other arts therapists and with other professionals such as psychologists and occupational therapists. They reported that it is an effective model and cited a number of reasons for this. They considered that better containment and consistency of approach were possible, and the opportunity to think together about the work was crucial because of the emotional impact it had. Because different individuals respond to different therapeutic approaches, clients benefit from the additional expertise and the expansion of creative approaches made possible. They also valued the increase in attention that can be given to individuals, and the relationships that can develop with individual therapists. Greater safety was a particularly important issue, as was the reduction of the therapists' sense of isolation. In addition, they felt that there were practical reasons that necessitated two therapists working together collaboratively.

Gafni and Hoffman (1991) cited fourteen beneficial reasons for working collaboratively. These included the training of inexperienced therapists; enhanced identification; greater awareness of transference and countertransference issues; recreation of a family setting; mutual supervision and feedback; combining complementary strengths and expertise; and continuity of care.

Conclusion

The difficulties art therapists face when working with people who have severe learning disabilities, autism and challenging behaviour are considerable. Therapists engage in prolonged and careful observation of their clients to understand their communication and to develop relationships with them, and are required to be highly skilled, sensitive, and tenacious. They have to work hard at maintaining boundaries, as their clients often have little understanding of what boundaries are, and yet they have to be flexible and creative. The slow pace of change the attacks on the therapist's thinking processes, the frequent risk to their safety and the negative impact of the countertransference all contribute to the exhaustion, frustration and sense of being de-skilled that therapists often experience despite their dedication to their work and their clients.

The collaborative model of therapy that I have presented here was developed as a response to the difficulties we faced in providing art, music and drama therapies to members of this client group, over a number of years. As a result of much hard work, we found it to be an effective therapeutic model that assists therapists to combat the difficulties they face in the course of long-term work with these clients. Long-term work is needed in many cases with clients who are severely learning disabled because of the slow pace of change and the frequent experience of loss of relationships that clients face, but can be hard for therapists to sustain.

The collaborative arts therapies model is synergistic in its effectiveness, greatly enhancing therapeutic gains made by the client. The focus of the work presented here was the image-making process, which facilitated the client's drawing development alongside the work on relationship issues and communication. The client's experiences of a 'parental couple', formed by a female and a male therapist working together, further enhanced the work that was possible, and significant therapeutic gains were evident.

Afterword

As a team my colleagues and I further developed this model, combining our creativity and expertise in collaborative work with different combinations of our art, drama and music therapy skills, and found the model to be increasingly effective. The skills and knowledge of our speech and language therapy colleague were invaluable in assisting us to develop modes of communication that were multi-dimensional, with less reliance on speech. Combining a behavioural approach (with an emphasis on enhancing communication) with a psychodynamic creative approach also seemed to be very effective in reducing challenging behaviour in our clients.

Our team worked intensively in the specialist unit for six years and, despite the satisfaction we experienced in our work, we also found it exhausting and debilitating. Therapy work with clients who are on the autistic spectrum, have a severe learning disability and display challenging behaviour is difficult and taxing for the therapist. Creative arts therapies can be accessible and effective for members of this client group. Good clinical supervision, supportive colleagues and managers and adequate infrastructures are all necessary for art therapists to thrive in their work. As NHS resources become more restricted in the current economic climate, arts therapists may find themselves working in inadequate conditions, thus making it more difficult to undertake the long-term work that is so beneficial for this client group. In any case, I think it is wise for arts therapists to hold a very small caseload of such challenging clients, and for that caseload to be balanced with other higher-functioning clients.

I hope this chapter has shown that a collaborative multi-arts approach works well for arts therapies with this client group when adequate support is in place.

References

Ashby, E. (2004) '"See how they run": a survey of the work of art therapists with people who have severe learning disabilities and challenging behaviour', unpublished Masters in Research in Art Psychotherapy Thesis, University of London: Goldsmiths College.

—— (2011) 'Resourceful, skilful and flexible: art therapy with people who have severe learning disabilities and challenging behaviour' in Gilroy, A. (ed.), *Art Therapy Research in Practice*, London: Peter Lang.

Bragge, A. and Fenner, P. (2009) 'The emergence of the "interactive square" as an approach to art therapy with children on the autistic spectrum', *International Journal of Art Therapy: Inscape*, 14 (1): 17–28.

Fox, L. (1998) 'Lost in space: the relevance of art therapy with clients who have autism or autistic features' in Rees, M. (ed.), *Drawing on Difference: Art Therapy with People who have Learning Difficulties*, London and New York: Routledge.

Gafni, S. and Hoffman, S. (1991) 'Teaching cotherapy: instructional and supervisory processes', *Journal of Contemporary Psychotherapy*, 21 (4): 285–89.

Hewett, D., Barber, M., Firth, G. and Harrison, T. (2011) *The Intensive Interaction Handbook*, London: Sage.

McGee, J., Menolascino, F., Hobbs, D. and Menousek, P. (1987) *Gentle Teaching: A Non-Aversive Approach to Helping Persons with Mental Retardation*, New York: Human Sciences.

Rabiger, S. (1998) 'Is art therapy? Some issues arising in working with children with severe learning difficulties' in Rees, M. (ed.), *Drawing on Difference: Art Therapy with People who have Learning Difficulties*, London and New York: Routledge.

Rostron, J. (2010) 'On amodal perception and language in art therapy with autism', *International Journal of Art Therapy: Inscape*, 15 (1): 36–49.

Stack, M. (1998) 'Humpty Dumpty's shell: working with autistic defence mechanisms in art therapy' in Rees, M. (ed.), *Drawing on Difference: Art Therapy with People who have Learning Difficulties*, London and New York: Routledge.

Tipple, R. (1992) 'Art therapy with people who have severe learning difficulties' in Waller, D. and Gilroy, A. (eds), *Art Therapy: A Handbook*, Buckingham: Open University Press.

Winnicott, D.W. (1971) *Playing and Reality*, Harmondsworth: Penguin Books.

Chapter 8

It is joy to be hidden but disaster not to be found

Art therapy with a girl diagnosed with autism

Ruth E. Jones

In the mid 1990s I was already working as an art therapist in a primary school for children with moderate learning difficulties and, with the opening of a specialist unit for autistic pupils, was asked to include some of these children on my caseload. In this setting, it was possible to work with young individuals for several years on a weekly basis with the support of the multi-disciplinary staff team. At the time it was still common to hear art therapy referred to as a 'young profession', and as there were almost no published accounts of working in art therapy with autistic children we created reflective discussion groups to think together about our work. Kathy Evans and Marijke Rutten-Saris were working on their Ph.D.s, looking into vitality affects and drawing development (RS-Index) respectively. Rita Simon and Marion Milner generously shared their decades of professional experience with us.

I turned to the writings of psychotherapists like Anne Alvarez (1992) who draws on the work of Bion, Anna Freud and Winnicott, and to Daniel Stern (1985), Frances Tustin (1990), D.W. Winnicott (1971), and Ken Wright (1991, 1998). My own developmental schema had been published (in Jacobs, 1998) and I benefitted from weekly supervision from pluralist psychotherapist Nina Farhi (1997). The triangulation provided by the unflinching support of the head teacher and my supervisor were vital in sustaining me in this work.

No matter how persuasive the theory one draws upon, there is no pre-established formula, no curriculum, for a therapy process and no two people are the same, whether autistic or not. Preconceived ideas can act like blinkers and limit our vision, both of the person before us and their art work. Understanding can only emerge from the unique experience created between the therapist and the other person, which at best is contextualised by pre-established theory. As an art therapist, I made myself and the materials available to each child to make use of in whatever way they needed and then drew upon all the registers I could muster (cognitive, somatic, theoretical, affective, metaphoric and imaginal, aesthetic) to 'pick up' and make some sense of what the child was expressing. This attitude of availability for experiencing required trust that a meaningful process would emerge between us over time.

I want to share some of the experiences, themes and questions that emerged over the course of a four-year art therapy process with a girl I shall call Elizabeth, who was 5½ when we began to meet weekly. She was the youngest of three siblings (her brother and sister both appeared free from any particular difficulties other than the demands of living with an autistic sibling). Elizabeth had suffered from perforated eardrums as an infant though by the time she underwent a brain stem hearing test aged 3 her hearing was found to be fine. She had no sense of danger and threw aggressive tantrums when challenged or frustrated. Elizabeth would only interact with her siblings on her own terms; otherwise she ignored them. Her parents struggled to make sense of their younger daughter and to manage her uncompromising behaviour. As can so often happen in relation to people with autism, the advice they received from the local CAMHS seemed strange and reactive: rather than seeking to understand the meaning of Elizabeth's frequent wish to bite her father, he was advised to get a folded tea towel to protect himself before letting her do it! Everyone was struggling and no one really knew what to do to help Elizabeth and her family in any meaningful way.

Elizabeth appeared to enjoy drawing and so was referred to art therapy when she had difficulty settling into the autism unit, where she was the only girl. She was a well-built and attractive child who could push, shove and bite (hard) when challenged. She didn't speak. In her presence I experienced an alienating sense of being with someone robustly fortified: like a castle, you might occasionally get a little look across the drawbridge but you were not allowed in. 'Stonewalled' was how it felt to be with her for much of the time. She seemed autistically defended rather than unformed, to use Tustin's distinction (1972: 17) and I was persistently struck by the impression that her mutism was in some way elective. Her parents thought Elizabeth learned by experience: it was frustrating that she persistently ignored them and frightening that they had to 'really mean it, and really feel it' to get her attention if she was ever in danger. During a series of assessments at 4½ she was found to have an above average IQ of 114 and to be already functioning at well over a 5-year-old level. It was not a question of intellectual impairment but one of preoccupation: Elizabeth's mind was focused elsewhere and other people's words and wishes usually didn't make it through to her.

The art therapy room was simple, with a sink set into a work-surface that ran the length of the far end of the room. Two tables formed a square in the middle of the room with several child-size chairs and my adult-size one; there was a water tray, a work-bench, a locked filing cabinet and a white board. The art materials were laid out on the work-surface to the left of the sink, with aprons and a large towel to the right. On the bench was a pile of different sized and coloured paper. I had devised a global timeline for the room, consisting of a long strip with large circles along its length. Blue circles designated future sessions. Any breaks and holidays were indicated by white circles and 'today' was marked with a sticker on the relevant blue circle. Before leaving on Fridays, I painted over the 'today' circle to make it 'the past', and stuck a new marker onto the next blue circle in preparation for the following week. This calendar, running the length of the room at ceiling level, had the advantage of working for everyone who used the room. Sessions lasted for half an hour and my one imposition was to insist that an apron was worn for painting: this requirement was to be a source of both conflict and contact with Elizabeth over the course of our working together.

Elizabeth's art therapy began with an initial four-week assessment. From the outset I felt impelled to use her full name and not the shortened versions, Liz or Lizzie, that everyone else used. In hindsight, this conveyed something of the principled discipline of the work we were embarking on where there could be no shortcuts. The following extracts from my notes give a flavour of the four assessment sessions:

> *First meeting:* ... an overwhelming sense of a thinking, reflective and coherent child who is choosing not to talk ... painted in red, black and blue while I held edge of her paper taut – she rested her hand on mine – hers was warm, mine cold ... she painted all over the paper ... understood my verbal comments made in unmodified language ... when I observed she was awkwardly pushing the paint onto the page, she changed her technique to pull the paint with the brush instead ... got paint on her hands so washed, removed apron and did some pencil drawing – spiral and 3 verticals and roof like horizontal before covering over with circular scribbles. Her dexterity, poise and purpose seemed very deliberate and purposeful.
>
> *Second meeting:* ... came readily from class and chose an apron, a chair and paints – began to paint with white then black and other colours mixed in ... laughed when I said she seemed to have to fill in all the gaps, and again when I noted that she was filling in the brown shape with black. She didn't cover the whole paper today. After painting she washed her hands and 'drove' the soap around the rim of the sink ... then started drawing – large circular forms then scribbled over them ... made hesitant verbalisation sounds throughout and also sang a little – sense of her having her own language.
>
> *Third meeting:* ... painted with yellow and blue and then with lots of black but some blank areas remained – today I felt affected by great sadness in her session, aware of feeling compassion and pathos ... drew two distinct spheres with black (Figure 8.1) and then another scribble drawing using four felt pens (yellow, red, blue and green).
>
> *Fourth meeting:* ... brought a pumpkin from class with her [it was nearly Halloween], and indicated she needed to go to the toilet on the way to the therapy room. Gave me her pumpkin to hold. Once finished, she ran ahead to the therapy room ... bright yellow painting became submerged in black and I experienced a weighty, sad mood. She made attempts to speak but I couldn't catch her meaning. She again drew with red, yellow, green and blue pens.

The four assessment sessions felt full of potential. Apparently motivated to attend the sessions and to engage with the materials, she made attempts to communicate directly with me, both verbally and through gesture. Her paintings were aesthetically pleasing (their form and beauty reminding me of Clyfford Still's 1953 oil paintings) and there seemed to be the beginning of a cumulative process

Figure 8.1 Early forms

in which she left a bit more space on the painted page each week. The way she painted with black inside the brown shape in the second session put me in mind of Tustin's analytic ideas about the autist's felt sense of a 'black hole' of 'not-being' (1990: 39). Elizabeth was also 'covering up' her drawings with scribble, providing a possible metaphor for her own hidden parts. She was able to elicit a lively emotional responsiveness in me, which Alvarez also experienced in her work (1992: 203). She evoked the feeling of hopefulness about her potential to become 'more fully alive as a human being', which Ogden (1989) saw as a vital motivating factor in a therapy. There was potential for symbolic meaning in her insistence on bringing and giving me the pumpkin to hold. Taking all these factors into account, and with the support of her parents and school staff, weekly art therapy sessions were included in Elizabeth's curriculum.

What follows is a sketch of some of the significant elements in the work. These are not exact, linear progressions or chronological stages but more like batches of themes, ebbing and flowing over a roughly cumulative process. Inevitably there were numerous possible strands of potential meaning to notice and invest with attention, and I had my 'personal signature' (Stern *et al.*, 1998) at that point in time, which meant that I 'saw' some things and 'missed' others. This account is largely un-theorised to leave the reader free to notice their own associations to the material.

Elizabeth quickly settled into a particular way of using her sessions. She would begin by painting a red face with coloured features, which she would always paint over with a mixture of paints, usually making a large brown or black patch on the otherwise empty page. It wasn't long before the calm and companionable atmosphere of the first sessions was replaced with one of exclusion and rigidity, where time and again my hopes that today, just maybe, the painted face would be allowed to remain, were disappointed. I began to feel increasingly useless and out of my depth as my lively, freethinking associations stalled and I experienced a creeping, soporific deadening of my ability to feel or think anything at all. This feeling state would accumulate as Elizabeth moved from painting to washing the brush in a full sink of water, turning it into a blue reflecting pool. She would insist I remain seated in my chair while I supposed she looked at her reflection in the water, and ineluctably my mind drained. It is almost impossible to convey how terrible, how soul destroying, is this feeling of being emptied of one's living mind and how helpless one is to prevent it happening. Despite my every effort to focus on any available fragments of potential meaning, it would overcome me, time and again, leaving me feeling coshed and utterly empty of anything mentally or emotionally satisfying or nourishing. After the promise of the assessment period, the sessions now seemed to be foundering in apparently unproductive repetitions. However, Elizabeth seemed to need my mindful attention and when it was lost to us both, she knew it and would do something to jolt me back into awareness, usually by going to damage something, or by flicking water at me or throwing something.

Figure 8.2 Emerging

After some time at the sink she would move back to the table and start drawing, bringing with her some temporary respite from the deadening affect. Typically she would draw a face with blue felt pen, initially as though emerging from water (Figure 8.2). Over the course of a year, these faces gradually developed club like arms with many stubby fingers, and eventually rudimentary legs but no bodies. Sometimes the drawings seemed to be of me as they included reference to the distinctive glasses I wore at the time, and sometimes they appeared to be a self-portrait as she had seen herself reflected in the sink of blue water. This pattern of systematic painting, absorption in water play and then tenuous drawing was accomplished week after week on a precarious knife-edge that could be disrupted at any time if Elizabeth felt impinged upon or upset by anyone or anything. Sometimes the requirement to wear an apron would 'set her off', and I learned that any reference to the absence of a body in her drawings would also send her into a violent rage (Tustin referred to the need to deny the body to avoid exposure to unbearable feelings of disembodiment [1990: 39]). She would 'blitz' the whole room, upsetting the tables, throwing the chairs, sweeping her folder and all its contents across the floor while I watched, awestruck, managing if I was lucky to stand between her and the art materials, otherwise they too would fly across the room. It might sound peculiar to say that I stood and watched as she was only a young child – why didn't I stop her and calm her down, contain the situation? In the sessions when Elizabeth was in a rage it was total and absolute, like a force of nature, and there was no way to intervene: like in a tornado, the only thing to do was to hold on and wait for the calm after the storm, to reassemble the room and hopefully resume some form of being together again.

Elizabeth sustained me in my belief that she was able to say more than she typically showed. Fairly early on, when I suggested as much, she made and held eye contact with me for a substantial time. At other times, she seemed to be speaking but her sounds were elusive and left me feeling unsure whether I had really heard her – for instance one day when I insisted she put on an apron before getting the paints, I thought I heard her say 'Shut up, stupid head', but couldn't be sure. However, about a year into the work, after the usual painting/water/drawing series, she took the clock from the shelf and sat cradling it in her lap and clearly said 'Happy'. Another time, when I again said I thought she could say more than she let on, she clearly counted up to five and back again as if to confirm my assertion. Into the second year, at the end of one particularly gruelling session of extreme blankness, she made use of part of my usual phrase for bringing the session to a close and, in a gentle, caring tone clearly said '... stop for today'. It was as if she was aware of how unbearable I was finding it.

For so much of the time it was very hard to sustain my active engagement with Elizabeth in the sessions. I easily felt like a useless lump, just imposing rules about wearing an apron for painting but unable to connect with her with any feeling. I identified with her parents and thought how hard it must be to have such a 'banishing' child, whose actions so often seemed simply intended to provoke reactions. In this affective climate, it was hard to remain attentive to the pockets of significant material that signalled an unfolding process, and supervision was vital in providing a forum for making meaningful connections, and thus making the raw experience thinkable.

It became clear that any breaks provoked a powerful reaction in Elizabeth, resulting in the room being blitzed in the subsequent session. As the work endured she started choosing larger sheets of paper for painting on, and while the red faces still disappeared under the brown and black over-painting, the larger space rhymed with a developing feeling of greater room for manoeuvre. It was as though she had more capacity to tolerate my presence as 'other'. One day she got paint on her finger and made a couple of finger prints to clean it off. I dared to pick up on this gesture and carefully, checking her expression to make sure it was ok, I made a couple of finger prints too. This developed into a tentative game over the next year or so where, after she had finished her painting, we would take it in turns to indicate where the other should put dabs of paint (Figure 8.3). On occasion, if the mood was right, she would squeal with laughter if I chased her finger with the brush on the page. She also became able to tolerate my joining her at the sink so that both our reflections were visible in the water, and she made cups containing differently coloured water that bobbed about in the blue pool.

Two years or so into the work, her blitzes came to be accompanied by a terrible sense of futility and dissatisfaction – no matter how hard she kicked the walls or threw the chairs and tables, it seemed to provide her with no relief. Similarly there were times when she seemed to run out of ideas, when her only apparent recourse

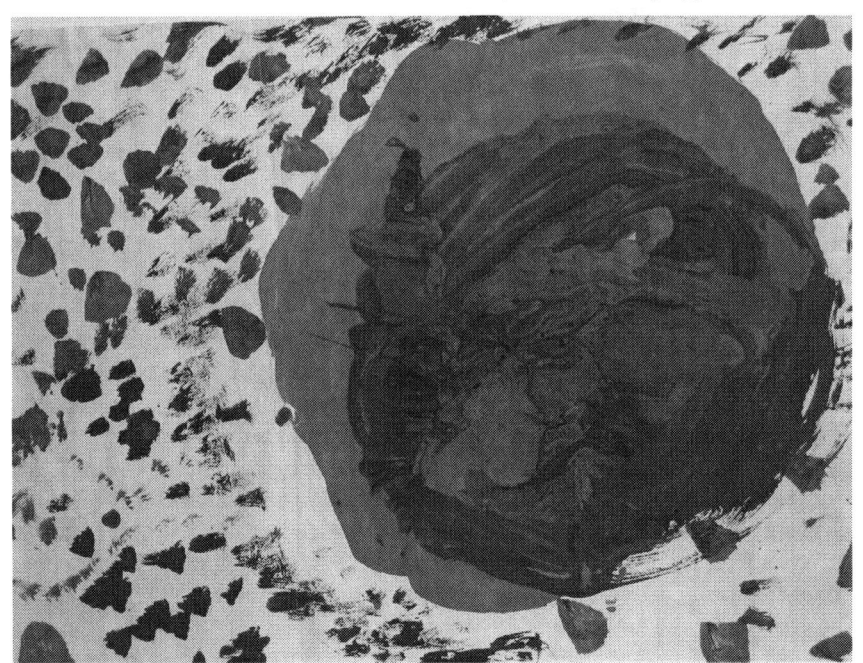

Figure 8.3 Over-painted face

was to 'get into a fight' about something. On one such occasion, I found the wherewithal to speak about how bad it feels when she doesn't know what to do, when nothing feels satisfying and we can't make it feel better. For a long moment she looked pensive and when I asked 'What is it Elizabeth?' she replied 'I don't know'. I affirmed that it is awful when we don't and she doesn't know. Her painting felt distracted and automatic that day and I sensed she would be able to bear me making an independent gesture. In an effort to reach out to her and try to give her something from elsewhere, from a separate mind of my own, I painted the words 'Hello Elizabeth'. She held long eye contact, and then prolonged this feeling of 'being together' by looking into the reflecting blue water so that we were in each other's company, separate but not too distant, looking at each other through the intermediary of the water. It was as if she was getting a feel for us being alongside each other in the container of the sessions.

For a period approximating to our third year, Elizabeth's art work was ephemeral – she didn't make any lasting images. Both the painting (over) faces and the associated interactive 'painting dots' game had ceased to feature. She continued to spend time making and playing with sinks full of coloured water and she only drew on and wiped the white board, leaving no image other than what I could hold onto in my memory. The moments of connection were not enough to assuage my doubts about the usefulness of working with Elizabeth in the absence of permanent artefacts. I was acutely aware of how much of the time there appeared to be no meaningful contact between us, and I felt inadequate to the task of being her therapist. I imagined that if I knew more, if I had a stronger grasp of 'analytic theory' or some other kind of knowledge, I might be able to respond meaningfully to the gestures she did make. I felt like a charlatan when colleagues were enthusiastic about her art therapy now that, in class, she was producing prolific drawings of Pokémon and other cartoon characters, animals and representations of places where she had been and things she had seen. Elizabeth was using representational drawing to augment her communication and her learning was progressing so well that she was going to begin integration out of the autism unit and into her year group in the main body of the school.

As we moved into our fourth year, her drawings on the white board became increasingly complex, including pairs of houses, multiple figures, numbers and strings of letters. She would sometimes write her name near the bottom of her image. One day she drew two figures, one tall with arms, legs and a body and the other small, stubby character with arms and legs attached to a smiling head. A mermaid began to feature frequently in her drawings. On another occasion, when everyone in the unit was exhausted by the relentless behaviour of a particularly challenging pupil, she came to the art therapy room and sat on the work-surface in a corner with the towel draped over her head. When I suggested that she was covering herself up to get some rest, like a bird in a cage, because she was finding it hard to cope with the other child's behaviour, she removed the towel and looked into my eyes with an extended, steady gaze. She then went to lie in the empty water tray, using the towel for a blanket and accepting the rolled up aprons from me for a pillow. After several minutes' companionable rest, she resumed her more usual use of the session.

Sometimes now she would tease me, pretending to take off her apron or making as if to climb into the water filled sink. After breaks she no longer blitzed the room but returned with enthusiasm and once even a hug. There were moments of real exchange and affection as she began to initiate turn-taking games, like winking and squinting, 'now you see me, now you don't' interactions. She would repeat her vocalisations to try to get me to understand her meaning, and tried out different kinds of eye contact. This was often uncomfortable as her explorations of close-up, sustained looking/staring into my eyes could feel clumsy and intrusive. But there was more trusting playfulness between us than ever before. For the first time she looked back through her folder at the accumulated history of the sessions in the form of the pictures and paintings I had carefully recovered each of the many times she had flung them all across the floor. She was sometimes also able to leave a picture unfinished and return to it the following week. I found that I was again able to experience recognisable, 'full' emotions in the sessions in place of the emptied-out, non-feeling states. I noted 'compassionate feelings: she strikes me today as being so lost and out of contact, not falling nor even floating just awfully out of touch' and 'a pleasure to be with; the moments of interactive engagement are no longer so frustratingly fleeting – more robust'. I was increasingly free to respond to her affectively – 'felt warm towards her today and wished she were a baby small enough to pick up and cradle'. Sometimes she would make me laugh out loud at her mannerisms and responses, and her affectionate gestures were delightful.

Elizabeth did not resume painting but she did start drawing on paper again. No longer just outlines, her work now involved complete, coloured-in figures and motifs. Some were reproductions of cartoon characters like the Pink Panther while others included her own symbolic leitmotifs such as the mermaid (Figure 8.4). As we were preparing to end our work together, she made an image of a flower in a pot with a watering can by its side on a solid ground (Figure 8.5). While she had been enjoying doing some gardening with her mother at the time, I feel sure (but of course cannot prove) that this parting image also had symbolic meaning in relation to the art therapy process where her growth and blossoming had been 'watered' within the process of the sessions. Similarly on her way to the final session she told me that she was 'wearing new shoes', which was the case, and which carried relational as well as metaphoric meaning. Her former frequent refusal to wear shoes had been a bone of contention in class and had sometimes been a theme in her therapy sessions but now she really did seem to be walking in new shoes as slowly but surely she fitted in socially and academically with her new school peer group.

The decision to bring Elizabeth's art therapy to a close was made when she was fully integrated into her new class in the main body of the special school. She had mastered significant developmental achievements, which I thought about in terms of Stern's four stages in the emerging sense of self (1985). Stern asserted that the

Figure 8.4 Mermaid and fishes

Figure 8.5 Flower and watering can

newborn's initial sense of an 'emergent self' is augmented by the 'sense of core self' for which the infant needs the integration of the four basic self-experiences (self-agency, self-coherence, self-affectivity and self-history) and which also includes the distinction between a sense of 'self *versus* other' and 'self *with* other'. The third stage, the 'sense of a subjective self', is where the infant discovers that he has a mind as well as other people having minds and the fourth stage, the 'sense of a verbal self', is when the ability to imagine or represent becomes possible in the child's mind and leads to the use of symbolism, in play and elsewhere. There are other theoretical concepts to articulate the progress made. For instance, in Winnicottian terms, she had mastered the capacity for play and playfulness, and she was now capable of feeling concern and making reparation in relation to whole objects, to use Kleinian Object Relations thinking.

What had the art therapy process got to do with Elizabeth's development? The distinguishing feature was that the time, space, materials and myself were all reliably available for her to affect and make use of, thus providing the transitional arena which Winnicott describes as the place in which 'doing' is suspended and the experience of 'being' can potentially emerge. This is vital when 'the need of the individual [is] to reach being before doing. "I am" must precede "I do", otherwise "I do" has no meaning for the individual ... It is an achievement' (Winnicott, 1971: 130). Thus Elizabeth had the opportunity to learn experientially about who she was rather than respond to the more usual learning situations which are primarily focused on developing new skills. In terms of Elizabeth's art work, using motifs that were not all evident in other settings, she had been able to repeat and work through the relational and drawing developments that I describe as follows:

1. The child sees (i.e. scans) and the therapist sees, separately.
2. The child looks, the therapist looks, separately.
3. The child allows the therapist to look at them (allows themself to be seen).
4. The child allows the therapist to see them looking. Use of art materials kinetically (sensation).
5. The child and the therapist looking at (and into) each other.
6. Development of reciprocity, dialogue of looking, watching and seeing.
7. Use of art materials symbolically (mark making). Development of play.
8. Use of art materials for representative work (image making). Development of language.

(Jones in Jacobs, 1998: 224)

I have made frequent reference to my own process of experiencing, feeling and thinking in relation to Elizabeth. I am somewhat wary about using the term countertransference because it can imply a one-way process of client impacting on or projecting into the therapist. I prefer the notion of intersubjective 'interpenetrating mix-up', which Balint (1968: 66) likens to the interplay of a fish and the sea where the two elements, here the therapist and client, affect each other in a continuous interplay. It could be said that for a long time Elizabeth's autistic defences served to disable the free flow of affect and 'mixing-up' between us. She could make an impact on me and my capacity to function while apparently keeping my impact on her to a bare minimum.

Winnicott stated that

> therapy takes place in the overlap of two areas of playing, that of the patient and that of the therapist ... The corollary of this is that where playing is not possible then the work done by the therapist is directed towards bringing the patient from a state of not being able to play into a state of being able to play.
> (Winnicott, 1971: 38)

I was allowing myself to experience things (including 'deadness' and 'non-feeling') in Elizabeth's presence without taking defensive action to protect myself from being affected by her (which would necessarily have diminished the 'space' available for her to use). Being available in this way affords a particular form of listening and makes understanding possible at pre-symbolic, indeed pre-representational levels of experiencing. Feeling heard and understood is crucial to any individual, and communications take place in many registers, which need to be received and digested affectively as well as intellectually. Elizabeth benefitted from experiencing herself over time in a potentially creative and potentially relational space where impingements were kept to a minimum. She was able to communicate and get me to know something about (non) feeling states that I had to bear in order to go on providing the potential space for her to enter into and make use of. The dual aspects of her art therapy, which are, first, the provision of resources, including the therapist, to affect and make use of, and, second, the availability of materials with a nature of their own for her to encounter and experience (again including the therapist), enabled Elizabeth to progress both developmentally and emotionally.

Afterword

It has been very difficult to re-engage with Elizabeth's art therapy more than ten years on. In preparing this account, I have been overwhelmed again by an inability to think and by excruciating feelings of emotional paralysis and internal depletion. The intersubjective process could not be put into words without being (re) experienced in the parts of myself that were psychologically engaged in the original work. As therapists we are deeply affected by our patients, as they are by us, and we have to make ourselves open and available to inter-psychic and intra-psychic processes if psychodynamic therapy work is to have substance. In this, there can be no shortcuts. There may be a great temptation to grasp hold of new research and theories that appear to offer a less demanding, more objective method, or standardised intervention model. As psychodynamic therapists, we have to metaphorically get into the water with the people we work with, and not stand on the periphery, keeping dry (Jones, 2010: 10–12). I believe that understanding is reached and developed through an ongoing interplay between affective experiencing and intellectual insight, that is, between affect and cognition.

There were several registers of psychological experiencing in Elizabeth's art therapy that contributed to the lessening of her autistic defences and to her overall progress. I have already referred to my own and Stern's conceptual frameworks for functional development and for the emergence of a sense of self. I suggest that both of these ways of seeing are relevant in Elizabeth's case. Furthermore, in the relative quiet of the non-directive sessions she was able to regress to less organised states of mind. This process of regression is encapsulated in her paintings, where a stereotypical face schema was relinquished for the undifferentiated 'mess' of the over-painting. It was at the moment of the over-painting in the sessions that I would experience the obliteration of my own mind. Whether this came about through an inter-psychic projective process (Elizabeth 'did it to me') or whether it was my own intra-psychic response to our particular intersubjective situation, I cannot say. Neuropsychoanalysts including Mark Solms are currently engaged in ground-breaking research into the organ of the human mind that has the potential to shed new light, in time, on inter-psychic phenomena of the kind I am referring to, and, potentially, could bring new neurological understanding to the condition of autism itself (Solms, 2011).

Be that as it may, art therapy gave Elizabeth a context and a 'medium' in which she could develop a primary awareness of 'being' and a sense of both her own selfhood and that of others. Reminiscent of Balint's image of a fish in the sea where the water and the living creature are intersubjectively intermingled, her mermaid (Figure 8.4) is in her element, and it is one that mediates her ability to make contact with others – there are little goldfish friends in her watery milieu. Elizabeth was now able to make tentative friendly connections with other children and could accept being involved in shared learning and play activities, instead of keeping herself apart. It seemed she was on track.

Postscript

The tragedy of Elizabeth's story is that when she transferred to secondary school, she was teased and bullied by older children. Some of the pupils who knew her from primary school tried to explain her vulnerabilities but staff didn't know how to make sense of her 'disproportionate' reactions. The primary school had learned how to engage with the needs of its autistic pupils but the cohort was only now reaching secondary age. This was a much larger school, educating children with a wide variety of moderate learning difficulties. Elizabeth refused to attend and the local authority refused to consider a change of provision. The family came under enormous strain, and only when they reached breaking point was it eventually agreed that she could attend a school for severe learning difficulties, which would provide more predictable routines and structures. Sadly, this left her without an appropriate peer group. Elizabeth received input from the staff, who enjoyed her higher ability in comparison with the other pupils, and she did learn new skills.

However, she had again come to rely on autistic defences. Behind a new fortification, a 'sound wall' that takes the form of a constant monotonous hum, she is protected but separated from others. The scope of her social interactions is limited despite her parents' best efforts to provide opportunities for her, and her repetitive, solitary pastimes cumulatively distance her from the ordinary world of others. Consequently her opportunities to learn relationally and from new experience are constricted and her emotional development has been curtailed. She has not had access to any further therapy.

So, we see the deep resonance in Elizabeth's case with Winnicott's words used in the title of this chapter: 'It is joy to be hidden but disaster not to be found' (Winnicott, 1965: 186).

References

Alvarez, A. (1992) *Live Company*, London: Routledge.
Balint, E. (1963) 'On being empty of oneself', *International Journal of Psychoanalysis*, 44: 470–80.
Balint, M. (1968) *The Basic Fault*, London: Tavistock.
Farhi, N. (1997) 'In the beginning there was darkness: images across the void', *Contemporary Psychoanalysis*, 44 (2008): 2–17.
Jacobs, M. (1998) 'Seeing and being seen in the experience of the therapist and the client', *European Journal of Psychotherapy and Counselling*, 1: 213–30, reprinted in (2008) *Our Desire of Unrest: Thinking About Therapy*, London: Karnac.
Jones, R.E. (2010) *Foreshoring the Unconscious: Living Psychoanalytic Practice*, Medway: Layfield.
Lanyado, M. (1994) *The Presence of the Therapist*, Hove: Brunner-Routledge.
Milner, M. (1969) *The Hands of The Living God*, London: Hogarth.
Ogden, T. (1989) *The Primitive Edge of Experience*, London: Karnac.
Rutten-Saris, M. (2002) 'The RS-index: an instrument for the Assessment of Interaction Structures in Drawing', Ph.D. dissertation, University of Hertfordshire.
Solms, M. (2011) 'The conscious Id', New York Lecture, Neuropsa. Online at: www.neuropsa.org.uk (accessed 8 January 2012).
Stern, D. (1985) *The Interpersonal World of the Infant: A View from Psychoanalysis and Developmental Psychology*, New York: Basic Books.
Stern, D.N., Sander, L.W., Nahum, J.P., Harrison, A.M., Lyons-Ruth, K., Morgan, A.C., Bruschweilerstern, N. and Tronick, E.Z. (1998) 'Non-interpretive mechanisms in psychoanalytic therapy: the "something more" than interpretation', *International Journal of Psycho-Analysis*, 79: 903–21.
Tustin, F. (1972) *Autism and Childhood Psychosis*, London: Hogarth.
—— (1990) *The Protective Shell in Children and Adults*, London: Karnac.
Winnicott, D.W. (1965, paper first published 1963) 'On communication' in *The Maturational Processes and the Facilitating Environment*, London: Hogarth.
—— (1971) *Playing and Reality*, London: Tavistock.
Wright, K. (1991) *Vision and Separation between Mother and Baby*, London: FAB.
—— (1998) 'Deep calling unto deep: artistic creativity and the maternal object', *British Journal of Psychotherapy*, 14 (4)(2008): 453–467 doi:10.1111/j.1752-0118.1998.tb00407.

Chapter 9

Adolescence and autonomy

Art therapy with a young adult with autistic spectrum disorder

Lesley Anne Moore

The following study describes six months of individual art therapy sessions with Simon (a pseudonym), a young man displaying autistic traits but without a formal diagnosis, who had recently begun to exhibit psychiatric problems. In the absence of a complete understanding of Simon's needs by the multidisciplinary team, I aim to describe his presentation within the framework of autistic spectrum disorder. I will outline the information known about Simon through his referral, to show how his early experiences and family background may have impacted upon his subsequent development and difficulties. I aim to present my understanding of the impairments that are a feature of his condition, and show how these have affected the quality of his life.

I will then present a description of the ways in which this client used art therapy to renegotiate his earliest developmental stages and simultaneously explore his burgeoning adult self, through his commitment to image-making and our therapeutic relationship.

Introduction

Simon is a young man whose parents were originally from Ghana. He had been newly referred to the Therapies Centre and not previously known to the Trust's Psychiatric/Learning Disability Services. I have described the complex nature of his referral as well as the clinical setting in which I worked with him. But first I intend to outline the issues and themes that I believe are pertinent to an understanding of the art therapy sessions.

Due to the possibility of Simon having autism I was expecting certain characteristics to be displayed as outlined in Kanner's (1943: 247–50) definition of the condition. My own preconceptions led me to imagine an interesting yet possibly slightly odd individual, locked into a world of his own, who may not have the inclination or capacity to communicate with others. I also wondered how art therapy might be used by an individual who may have 'difficulty in using symbols and with developing the imagination' (Fox, 1998: 74).

Despite Simon's age at the time of his referral (20 years old), I will be presenting his situation as bound up within the state of adolescence due to the pervasive effects of his condition on his emotional development and the difficulties of separation from his mother. It became apparent that his mother had difficulty letting go and naturally wished to protect him. Bungener and McCormack (1994: 368) maintain that this 'intense relationship, which is normal in the neo-natal and infant period, can persist for years when a child is disabled'. This situation can be made more complex when the child is autistic, due to a particular feature of their condition being a merging of the stages of development, so that for the autistic client, the earliest experiences can be understood to co-exist with their current developmental stage. Tustin (1992: 35) suggests that the autistic child's 'awareness of bodily separateness is not experienced in slow and manageable degrees, as is the case in normal development; it comes suddenly and traumatically'.

For Simon this meant that within the images produced during art therapy and through our therapeutic relationship, he seemed to be re-negotiating his earliest experiences of feeding as well as attempting to explore the process of leaving childhood behind and becoming independent. Adolescence is usually a time of establishing peer relationships, developing sexuality and separation from the family. Yet for the learning disabled client who is unable to live independently these processes are harder, if not impossible, to overcome. Sinason (1992: 189) describes the terrible predicament that Simon might be going through when 'the person who cannot deal with your feelings is also the person from whom you need reassurance because of your own attachment needs'.

The setting

The art therapy department was based at a therapeutic services centre for people with learning disabilities ranging from profound special needs to mild cognitive impairments. As well as providing day support, the centre offered a variety of therapies and clinical approaches to treatment. The art therapy room, available for group and individual sessions, was a well-established creative space. There was a registered art therapist with a particular interest in working with clients with autism. She was my clinical supervisor within the placement, and had opened up avenues for thinking about this client's images and developmental state of mind, as well as sharing my pleasure at his progress.

Referral

Simon was referred by the SHO (senior house officer) to his consultant. The referral form stated that his 'most likely diagnosis' was autistic spectrum disorder with obsessional features, that he was recently troubled by obsessive thoughts regarding cleanliness, and he was also described as low in mood. Simon enjoyed drawing at home, the referral stated, but had difficulty expressing himself so it was felt that art therapy might be 'a good medium for this'. He had recently completed a course with an employment training college and had started attending a work-focused day centre for two days per week. My initial impression from this referral was of a motivated and fairly able individual.

Simon's medical file was sparse, containing only a brief report from the SHO who had recommended a full psychological assessment as so little was known about him, but she was able to provide some interesting facts in her brief outline of Simon's life.

Family history

Simon lived with his mother and two of his siblings. I was particularly struck by the fact that he has a twin sister who is currently studying at university. The twins were born prematurely and required treatment in a special care baby unit, indicating that problems at the time of birth and with subsequent attachment were possible. Simon was slow to reach his developmental milestones. His father died when Simon was only 5 years old, and from that age he had been in receipt of specialist educational services. At age 7 he had entered mainstream education but was bullied and unable to cope with the educational demands, so returned to specialist schools until the age of 16. He then attended local colleges until the age of 19, and was described as more withdrawn in the year since leaving college.

He was described as quiet and isolated, finding it difficult to share his feelings; presenting with very little spontaneous speech, though he would respond politely to questions. Having lost his father at a young age, he seemed to have spent a great deal of time in the company of his mother and sisters. His mother claimed that he never initiated physical contact.

During the previous couple of months he had experienced night terrors, believing that the bedclothes touching his body were vampires attacking him. There was a query as to whether Simon was psychotic and experiencing hallucinations or nightmares; Simon had described his experiences as 'foolish thoughts'. Wing (1981: 122) queries whether autism is a psychotic process or a stable personality trait or disorder.

Apart from his increasing withdrawal and depressed mood, he had been referred to the consultant because of strange behaviours observed by his mother, in particular an increasing reluctance to eat. He had recently expressed the belief that people would 'do something to his mind' if he put food in his mouth; that if he ate in front of others they would be able to read his thoughts. He was described as guarded and suspicious in his manner.

I arranged for six to eight individual assessment sessions, initially lasting 45 minutes, followed by a review. I hoped to gain some understanding of Simon's quality of life and to provide him with a safe space to explore his experience of the world. The overall treatment aim was to build a trusting relationship to enable him to communicate more fully in order that he may be able to lead a less isolated and less fearful life.

The art therapy sessions

Shall I start now?

My first meeting with Simon was in the reception area of the Therapies Centre where he was waiting with his mother. He immediately smiled at me, yet was hesitant in his manner, as is natural when meeting someone for the first time. I was aware of an eagerness in his expression, and was reminded of Sinason's concept of a 'handicapped smile' (1992: 148–9) that attempts to smooth over the fear of showing damage to others. Physically, Simon was young for his age, with a slight, boyish physique, a neat appearance and a gentle manner. At almost 21 he was still some way from manhood, and seemed unsure of his sexuality, almost feminine. He appeared studious and fragile and it was easy to imagine him as the target of school bullies.

Having been prompted by his mother, he followed me up the stairs. She made as if to follow, and when I suggested that she wait in reception she seemed surprised and disappointed at not joining us. It did not seem to have occurred to her that the session was not to involve her as well as her son, though understandably she may have not known what to expect when bringing him for the first time. My impression of Simon's mother, through this meeting and our telephone conversations, was that she had quite an anxious disposition and that the responsibilities of bringing up her family as a lone parent had taken its toll on her health and peace of mind.

Once in the art therapy room Simon appeared curious but slightly over-polite, even formal in his manner. He said that he did not know that he was coming to art therapy today and I was surprised that his mother had apparently not informed him of this appointment, despite my having confirmed arrangements with her by telephone the week before, following letters sent to them both.

As an introduction, I suggested various ways that he might choose to use these sessions, inviting him to use the art materials, to talk or think about things together. We then sat comfortably in silence for a while, until eventually he asked, 'Shall I start now?' as if asking permission, and then 'What shall I paint?' When I asked him what sprang to mind he said, 'I'll draw myself sitting down', and began by very carefully copying his own arm. He painted the figure slowly and with great concentration, paying particular attention to achieving the appropriate brown skin tones on the hands and face. When finished he held the image out for me to look at and I saw that the figure he had painted appeared to be rigidly leaning and almost falling off a bench wearing quite a startled expression. The eyes were wide open and fearful-looking. As a representation of self this was clearly not a person at ease in his body or relaxed in the world.

Later that day, during supervision, we looked at Simon's image and my supervisor observed a fairly prominent feature that I had not noticed earlier: the figure appeared to be holding in his hand an erect phallus. This form had appeared in the paint marks, and though I had not noticed its emergence during the session, was clearly visible. It led me to question whether he was unconsciously exposing his sexuality within the image, and was revealing a side of himself that needed to be explored. Perhaps he was unconsciously expressing the need to 'play' with himself (both within the therapeutic process and as a masturbatory phantasy), and having been in a sense 'caught in the act' (the startled expression and posture), was unsure whether it was safe to do so in my presence. Had I been unaware of this unconscious sexual element within his work due to his almost asexual presentation?

A few weeks later, whilst looking through his folder of art work, he examined this image of the seated figure and described it as 'a person sitting on a chair'. I said that I had thought it was of himself but he shook his head and stated: 'No, it's just a person'. Having looked at it again with fresh eyes he seemed to disown the aspect that was his own identity. Perhaps he was unconsciously disassociating himself from the exposure of male sexuality revealed within it, or was uncomfortable about identifying himself with some element or feeling expressed. It may have just been too soon for him to own the sense of fear or unease that the image evoked.

About to eat?

During the next session Simon had selected a pencil but before continuing asked me, 'What shall I draw?' I asked what he had been thinking about that day and he said, 'I'll draw myself, eating an apple', and began to copy his own hand. The completed drawing was not of a person eating an apple but of a hand holding an uneaten whole apple. I suggested to him that in the drawing he was not yet eating but about to take a bite, and he agreed. When colouring it he described how apples were different shades of green, and red too, leading me to expect that he would colour his apple this way, but he had chosen to use just one rather dark shade of green, which resulted in the apple having an unripe appearance. I asked him what kind of an apple it was. He thought for a moment and responded, 'Nice and juicy'. I agreed, keen to encourage and support his efforts, though privately I thought it appeared to be an undeveloped piece of fruit, yet to benefit from the sun.

As we spoke about the nature of the apple, I felt that we were also talking about Simon himself and his art therapy sessions; that he was about to enter into something which could be tasty and nourishing or sour and unpleasant, and that he was a young man on the brink of adulthood (in a sense also unripe), afraid yet intrigued. I could not help associating the apple with the offer of temptation and original sin, and wondered what the consequences of taking a bite might be for him.

I was aware that our conversation allowed for a symbolic handling of the ideas contained within Simon's image. His use of imagery enabled discussions to take place on several levels that would not have been possible if we were relying purely on verbal dialogue. Apparently simple objects and ideas were introduced naturally that both broadened and deepened our communication in a way that Simon did not seem to find threatening. In fact he clearly derived enjoyment and satisfaction from his efforts as well as our discussions about them. A therapeutic intervention without imagery certainly would not have revealed such a rich source of material, or the possibilities to explore and work through these complex subjects with him.

After three assessment sessions I realised that the 45-minute sessions that I had originally offered Simon were not long enough and that we would both benefit from some extra time. I was considering this when Simon himself requested a 'longerer' time, so his sessions were extended to one hour.

Skin

During the following session he drew 'a person eating an ice cream', which was in fact a hand holding an ice-cream cornet. He examined the skin colour on his hands and in the picture for some time, using pink and brown felt-tip pens to achieve the right colour contrast to match his own hand colour, yet coloured the hands predominantly pink with brown lines to represent the creases in his skin. The ice cream was depicted as very dark brown – 'Chocolate flavour, my favourite', he explained. I felt that in this image he might be exploring the boundary of self that was his skin, as well as his own racial identity. He seemed to be examining his skin, in particular its colour, as if for the first time. Tustin (1992: 35) observes that when autistic children 'begin to sense that they have a skin, they feel that they are inside something which makes them feel safe'.

I noticed a couple of quirky vocal mannerisms, which revealed his difficulty in responding when he was lost in his own thoughts. He would occasionally change his mind when answering me and say 'No, meant to be yes' or 'Yes, meant to be no'. If I asked him a question which he did not hear or understand he would frequently say 'Who?' as others might say 'What?' or 'Pardon?' This led me to think about Williams' (1998: 13) descriptions of the states of being which she calls the modes of 'all self, no other' and 'no self, no other'. Was it hard for him to be in the presence of others and maintain a sense of himself as distinct and separate? As a twin had he never felt truly individual?

During the next session Simon made three images, including a drawing in brown pencil of a peeled banana, followed by a drawing of a brown hand holding a peeled banana. He was quite particular and assertive in his search amongst the box of coloured pencils for what he called a 'regular' one that was a dark enough shade of brown, describing the finished colour of the hand as like his own, and that he was very pleased with it. During the making of these images Simon frequently asked me to look at what he had drawn, enquiring: 'What does it look like?' It seemed important to him that the making of these images were to be witnessed, recognised and described by someone else.

Although Simon enjoyed making art work at home, this process was different, and he clearly derived extra support, satisfaction and meaning from the sessions. As the rapport between us developed, he became noticeably more at ease in conversation and in expressing his needs. I recognised the importance of my role in witnessing and acknowledging the creation of his images, as well as thinking about and reflecting with him on their content and meaning.

Many of the images made during our sessions contained the idea of someone not eating yet but just about to, frozen in the moment prior to an action, or in preparation for it. I continued to be struck by the feeling that Simon was on the verge of adulthood, but caught or stuck in the moment just before he was able to take a bite out of life.

Though he would not elaborate on why he had come to see 'the doctor' (psychiatrist) about his eating, he frequently spoke about food as well as depicting it in his images. He liked to describe his favourite foods, would ask me about mine, and said that at the social clubs he would like to attend regularly he wished he could 'dance and eat and listen to music with mates'.

I reflected on the significance of food and feeding, about the act of putting outside stuff into oneself for nourishment and pleasure, the annihilation of hunger and, ultimately, survival. I also wondered about Simon's (ongoing?) delusional belief that if he put food in his mouth then others might be able to read his thoughts, and considered the impact of this on his art therapy sessions. Was the food in his images uneaten so that I would not be able to gain access to his mind? His reluctance to eat prior to his referral, his frequent depictions and interest in food yet inability to eat within the life of his images indicated the significance of his ambivalence towards food and feeding. Could there have been too much intrusion or impingement in his earliest experiences, possibly as a result of a natural tendency towards over-protection on the part of his loving but anxious mother?

Nevertheless I felt positive about the images, for it seemed possible that within them he might be 'preparing to eat' in my presence, thereby containing the possibility of allowing me into his world. It seemed to me that they also revealed Simon's potential to face and explore his fears, and hopefully to work through them.

Someone eating

In the next session Simon said that he would draw 'a person eating a hamburger'. Once again the 'person' was actually his own hand, floating disembodied on the paper. But the hand appeared as a devouring mouth trying to eat the burger rather than just holding it. Simon was again choosing to confront his fears around eating and being intruded on (by others reading his thoughts?) through his imagery. The hand in the image had a threatening appearance and seemed to be on the point of devouring the food rather than holding it in preparation for eating.

He also returned to the subject of 'someone eating a banana'. But this image was different: this was of someone actually eating instead of just about to, and he had included a head instead of just hands. It was a curious image and quite frightening, perhaps even psychotic looking. The figure's teeth were bared in its large open mouth, and the banana with its peeled back skin looked like the body of a centaur belonging to the head, or perhaps the body, of a figure whose head had been devoured by the larger head.

In order to try to understand Simon's ambivalent relationship with food and his mother I found it helpful to think about Melanie Klein's theories concerning early object relations. She describes the object-world of the child as consisting of hostile and persecuting or else gratifying parts of the real world (Mitchell, 1991: 141). The baby's earliest experiences relate to the primary care-giver through feeding: it has hunger pains, which alongside the frustrations and difficulties of feeding are associated with this first object, as well as the comfort and relief it provides. Thus there are destructive as well as loving feelings towards one and the same object and this may give rise to deep and disturbing internal conflicts. It was clear that Simon, though almost an adult, continued to experience difficulties overcoming these desires and fears. As he continued to be reliant on his mother, did he also find it intolerable to contain feelings of resentment, even unconscious anger, towards her?

Klein states that difficulties with eating often have a paranoid root (Mitchell, 1991: 118, 127) and that there are often further anxieties and inhibitions around ingesting substances perceived as destructive. Kanner also reflects on the difficulties that an autistic infant might experience with food, which he describes as 'the earliest intrusion brought to the child from the outside' and maintains that for these hyper-sensitive children everything that is brought from the outside 'represents a dreaded intrusion' (1943: 244).

Can I come back for more?

One week Simon decided to draw then paint 'myself, eating a cake'. He made two versions of these, saying that the first attempt had 'gone a bit wrong'. The cake grew larger as he repainted it, seeming to change his mind about the shape several times and striving to 'get it right'. I watched him paint and it looked as if he was removing the slice and then returning it to the cake, then deciding to take it out again, as if not sure whether or not to take a piece. Both versions of this image ended up with a large chunk having been removed from the cake and smaller pieces being taken by the hands. The pieces of cake removed by the hands were smaller slices than the gaps left behind, yet they remained 'uneaten'.

Simon chose red paint to fill in the nails on both hands, and seemed particularly pleased with this aspect of his work. 'I like the way I've done the nails', he kept saying as he finished both pictures, deliberately drawing attention to this aspect of his hands' appearance.

One week he drew an image of a person riding a bike, from the viewpoint of looking down at the handlebars from above the head. The image looked like someone lifting weights, with a tiny head in the middle, the main focus once again the hands and arms. He told me that he used to have a red bicycle like this one but it had been stolen, which he seemed regretful but resigned about. Following this he spoke of other losses: that all of his siblings had attended university, and that he was the only one who hadn't, and the many changes in his life that he did not understand.

He told me that he really liked painting and hoped that he would be able to carry on. I asked if he meant continuing to come here or painting in the years to come and he repeated the latter. It seemed that he could not take anything he enjoyed for granted and was worried about losing it. When that session ended he appeared sad, as if he did not want to let go. I asked him if it was hard to leave today and he replied with a lengthened yes, as if he was saying something he shouldn't. Then he asked, 'I can come back next week, can't I?'

First steps

When I went downstairs to reception to collect Simon for his next session he was standing alone looking pleased with himself, with a huge smile on his face. I looked around to greet his mother but could not see her. Simon saw me glancing around and announced, 'I came on my own today!'

Once upstairs he revealed the circumstances leading up to this breakthrough. Due to the rainy weather his mother had decided that they would not be coming. He said that she was about to phone but Simon had 'insisted' that he wanted to come today, so had travelled on his own to the centre for the first time. This involved a walk, a bus, a tram and another walk so was not a straightforward journey by any means. It felt as though he was asserting his independence and striking out on his own.

His appearance was also altered and I felt that he looked less boyish. He had had his hair cut in a short style with a parting shaved into the front at an angle, a style I had noticed in more streetwise young black men. He said that his older brother had given him the haircut, and I realised that this was the first time that he had mentioned his brother (who was nine years older than Simon), even though he also lived at home with mum. Simon had never mentioned his father or this older brother before.

As if to coincide with his progress in travelling independently, Simon enthusiastically announced that he would be drawing something different from eating, as he had done 'too many cakes'. He said that he would be drawing 'athletics' instead of food and today would try 'a person running'. He struggled with his new subject, attempting to draw a figure in motion from memory, and told me that he was 'really thinking' about it. He erased several attempts, clearly not content with his efforts, rubbing out a larger figure entirely and ending up with several smaller ones, all with their arms outstretched, giving the appearance of relay runners.

Simon's new choice of subject matter depicted a sport dominated by black role models. For a young man without much male influence in his life I felt that this was a positive change for his self-esteem. In supervision we were struck by the idea of him metaphorically 'taking the baton' from his older brother, as if he was finally ready to step into manhood. It seemed that Simon was identifying with a male member of his family for the first time, and possibly recognised that within the family he was now the next 'man in line'. The move away from his mother, by travelling to the session independently, was an indication of his progress. I entertained the image of Simon running as if liberated into a new stage of his life, and asked Simon what stage of the race the runners were at. He said that they were 'just beginning'.

Who's the boss?

I was pleased when Simon maintained his progress by once again travelling by himself the following week. I said that he seemed to be more independent now and he asked me what this meant. I described him making decisions and travelling on his own and he appeared to be intrigued by the meaning of the word as if it was a new concept to him.

He sat looking thoughtfully at the paper for a while and I asked if he was thinking about a subject to draw. He asked me what the word 'subject' meant, and I suggested that it could be the idea he had for a drawing and his face lit up in recognition. I felt that he liked this thought – that his drawings had meaning and subject matter, and perhaps that he himself was responsible for the idea behind them.

He wanted to try another drawing of athletics, and again drew figures running along a racetrack. As the drawing took shape he again rubbed out as much as he drew, and he appeared to be concentrating hard. Having struggled with his running figures he then began to work more freely as he filled in the background, sketching in the crowd watching the race in a loose, easy manner. I suggested to him that sometimes it was easier to draw when you are not so worried about making it perfect and he agreed, saying that the voice telling him that his drawing 'had to be perfect' was like listening to someone 'whinging' inside his head. He was able to compare this with the pleasure he felt when his drawing was going well, remembering this feeling of satisfaction as 'Yippee!'

I thought about the amount of pleasure he clearly derived from using art materials and wondered whether this was to do with the autonomy he experienced. I returned to the subject of independence by suggesting to him that he was 'in charge' when he made a drawing in that he chose the idea and made choices about how it would look. He was in fact 'the boss' when he was making a drawing. He looked amused and shook his head, exclaiming, 'No – you're the boss!' I pointed out that he made the drawings without my help, and made every decision about their contents, therefore who was the boss? 'But you teach me', he suggested. I denied this, explaining that we talked together about his art work, but that I had not made any suggestions as to how or what he should draw or paint. So, who was the boss here? He seemed delighted and we were both laughing when he finally declared, 'I am!'

Conclusion

During the last week of his art therapy Simon started voluntary work, and was pleased to report that his first day helping with a charity had gone well. He had managed to travel to the Saturday Social Club independently on several occasions.

He was also looking forward to starting a computer course, and appeared to be doing well generally with no noticeable weight loss.

My clinical supervisor had considered this case to be potentially fraught with difficulty as it involved complex presenting features, including eating problems that have the capacity to be life-threatening. She shared my delight at Simon's development and progress, and that the outcome of this intervention was so promising.

So what were the important elements that enabled Simon to begin the process of self-healing and start to overcome his fears? Simon's willingness to approach art making as an exploratory process and his lively engagement with the art materials and his images were a crucial factor, involving courage and commitment. The therapeutic relationship that quickly developed into a warm rapport also allowed for the therapeutic process to develop in a relatively short space of time. The physical environment of the therapy room, being a designated art therapy space, also provided an appropriate creative setting free from interruption, and this allowed for the companionable yet serious atmosphere of the sessions to develop and bear fruit.

This study also shows the importance of context, and the effectiveness of constant evaluation through reflective practice and supervision throughout the work. It was essential to keep in mind issues relating to his possible early experiences, his position within the family and ethnic background, as well as his development as a young man, in order for me as a white female trainee therapist to attempt to appreciate his situation. Within this context it was then vital to stay open to the potential meanings of the rich material Simon brought to his sessions.

I did not believe at any point that Simon's autistic traits prevented him from using his art therapy sessions effectively or inhibited his ability to use art materials in an imaginative, symbolic way. I think that he was able to use and grasp a wider range of ideas through his image-making than if he had been engaged in a purely verbal form of psychotherapy, and would have been more constrained or guarded without the process and product of art making.

The therapeutic relationship and the 'potential space' (Winnicott, 1986: 75) created within it through the sharing of Simon's images gave him the opportunity to explore his sense of self. Winnicott (1986: 66) describes how, if the conditions are right in therapy, 'the individual can come together and exist as a unit, not as a defence against anxiety but as an expression of I AM. I am alive, I am myself'. I hope that Simon's art therapy provided the right conditions to allow him to take the first step of this journey towards independence and adulthood. I also hoped that Simon continued to enjoy a more independent lifestyle free from morbid fears. And that eventually he was able to dance and eat and listen to music with his friends whenever he chose.

Afterword

The process of examining a clinical study written as part of my art therapy training has been a curious one. Since the time of writing I have been a practising art therapist for over ten years working in adult mental health, and have also become a mother, so I am looking back from a very different viewpoint. I now feel more empathy towards Simon's mother, who brought up a large family as a single parent and clearly struggled with her own health and well-being. Simon's art therapy sessions had an impact on her that I did not fully appreciate at the time. She must have found it a considerable effort to escort him each week without a car, and clearly struggled with this, when perhaps she lacked support for herself. My subsequent clinical practice has led to a much greater awareness of the importance of working collaboratively with carers, and the value of family-orientated approaches. In retrospect, I speculated about her role in his difficulties but was not confident about involving or engaging her in the process itself. Carer's assessments are now routinely offered, and can identify and address needs that subsequently also benefit the service user. Had I been able to engage her in the process, she may also have been in a position to answer some of the many unanswered questions I had about fundamental changes involving his eating and sleep difficulties.

Although Simon appeared to have made progress in many ways, and seemed much less anxious than when I first started working with him, it was not clear whether he continued to experience paranoid or delusional thoughts. I can see from my process notes that he eventually began to drink, and even eat a biscuit, in my presence but I did not determine whether his psychotic symptomatology had significantly altered. In retrospect, it should have been an essential aspect of the ending of this work to gain an understanding of the changes in Simon's underlying mental state, but as a trainee therapist I focused on positive changes in his behaviour and presentation.

In my subsequent clinical practice I have worked with many individuals who have Asperger's Syndrome, referred through mental health services, rather than through learning disability services which tended to be the case 10 years ago when less was understood about individuals with high-functioning autism.

The person-centred approach I instinctively followed with Simon relates well to the more recent work of Bromfield, who offers a model of 'relationship-based therapy' with children and adolescents with Asperger's (Bromfield, 2010: xiii). He describes the young people he works with as needing more than anything a 'connection to others, and to themselves', which is the aspect I believe Simon valued so much about his sessions. Bromfield also regards engaging with parents as essential, in order to shed light on both the inner and shared life of their child. He reminds therapists that some, like Simon's mother, 'may experience Asperger-like anxieties, fears and limitations that need our caring attention' (Bromfield, 2010: 17).

References

Bromfield, R. (2010) *Doing Therapy with Children and Adolescents with Asperger Syndrome,* New Jersey: John Wiley.

Bungener, J. and McCormack, B. (1994) 'Psychotherapy and learning disability' in Clarkson, P. and Pokorney, M. (ed), *The Handbook of Psychotherapy,* London: Routledge.

Fox, L. (1998) 'Lost in space: the relevance of art therapy with clients who have autism or autistic features' in Rees, M. (ed.), *Drawing on Difference: Art Therapy with People who have Learning Difficulties*, London and New York: Routledge.

Hughes, R. (1988) 'Transitional phenomena and the potential space in art therapy with mentally handicapped people', *Inscape*, summer: 4–8.

Kanner, L. (1943) 'Autistic disturbances of affective contact', *Nervous Child*, 2 (244): 247–50.

Kuczaj, E. (1998) 'Learning to say "goodbye": loss and bereavement in learning difficulties and the role of art therapy' in Rees, M. (ed.), *Drawing on Difference: Art Therapy with People who have Learning Difficulties*, London and New York: Routledge.

Mitchell, J. (ed.) (1991) *The Selected Melanie Klein*, Penguin Books.

Rostron, J. (2010) 'Amodal perception and language in art therapy with autism', *International Journal of Art Therapy: Inscape*, 15 (1): 36–49.

Segal, H. (1988) 'Notes on symbol formation', *The Work of Hannah Segal*, New York: Aronson Press.

Sinason, V. (1992) *Mental Handicap and the Human Condition: New Approaches from the Tavistock*, London: Free Association Books.

Stack, M. (1998) 'Humpty Dumpty's shell: working with autistic defence mechanisms in art therapy' in Rees, M. (ed.), *Drawing on Difference: Art Therapy with People who have Learning Difficulties*, London and New York: Routledge.

Stott, J. and Males, B. (1984) 'Art therapy for people who are mentally handicapped', in Dalley, T. (ed.) *Art as Therapy*, London and New York: Tavistock/Routledge.

Tipple, R. (1994) 'Communication and interpretation with people who have a learning disability', *Inscape*, 2: 31–5.

Tustin, F. (1992) *Autistic States in Children*, London and New York: Tavistock/Routledge.

Williams, D. (1998) *Autism and Sensing: The Unlost Instinct*, London and Philadelphia: Elizabeth Kingsley.

Wing, L. (1981) 'Asperger's Syndrome: a clinical account', *Journal of Psychological Medicine*, 11: 115–29.

Winnicott, D.W. (1986) *Playing and Reality*, Harmondsworth: Pelican Books.

Chapter 10

Contemporary views and ways forward for future practice

Theoretical shifts: the new century

In 2001 in the USA Kellerman focused on the art produced by people on the autistic spectrum. She points out the prevalence of 'pre-attentive' images, which she links to 'that part of the vision process that occurs an instant before one's brain finishes adding colour to its representation, identifying what is before the eyes, and moves to conceptual considerations – and the stored, simplified descriptions of the object' (2001: 22). She suggests that this is because autistic people are not 'culturally aware', which we suggest is similar to not being aware that other people have different minds. Kellerman is not describing work produced in art therapy, but her observations resonate with the work detailed by Wilson and Byers.

At the same time, in the UK, Evans and Dubowski published *Art Therapy with Children on the Autistic Spectrum* (2001), which formulates an approach called 'interactive art therapy'. This is based on theories such as Stern's (1985) and, from videoing the children's interactions, Evans and Dubowski conclude that autistic children do approach others but retreat when the response is overwhelming or over-stimulating. They recommend video-recording the first art therapy session and looking for the minute cues that cause the autistic child to retreat. Thus the art therapist can modify her own behaviour and interact with the child through the art materials, increasing stimuli where and if possible, in order to enable the child to progress in his development.

In the same year Henley elaborated on his observation that children with Asperger's Syndrome tend to depict 'annihilation fantasies', which can be linked to their 'impairment in reality testing' (2001: 114). He advises that the art therapist offer 'softer interpretations' that are reality based. Thus Henley linked one of his client's frightening drawings of inter-planetary collisions to the fantasy of the *Star Wars* trilogy (2001: 117). He then 'reminded him that he and his family enjoyed' going to see these films in the safety of the cinema. Henley recommends longer-term work, of an average of one and a half years, to allow for a working through of 'annihilation anxiety'.

Conversely, in 2008 Tipple provided a model for a brief art therapy intervention of twelve weeks, recognising that short-term work is what is available in some organisations. He recommends 'close observation and attentiveness to small changes', focus and activity on the part of the therapist (Tipple, 2008). In the same book Patterson shows how the use of art materials and images makes interaction safer for these children, because they can regulate the directness of their contact with the art therapist, and she shows that it is possible for them to 'develop a mechanism for thought' (Patterson, 2008: 128). Meyerowitz-Katz also emphasises this factor and describes how it can facilitate 'the growth and development of the internal world' (Meyerowitz-Katz, 2008: 248).

Meyerowitz-Katz shows how easily a child with Asperger's can feel overloaded by the therapist. She describes a process of containment in which she tells the client what she sees her doing in order to 'validate' the client's experience and give her a sense 'of being seen, and of being the focus of someone else's mind' (Meyerowitz-Katz, 2008: 245). Meyerowitz-Katz's example illustrates a perceptible shift from Tipple's description of interpretation as 'the communication of understanding and the sharing of insights with the patient' (Tipple 1994: 32) to an emphasis on what can actually be seen or observed.

In his more recent chapter, Tipple (2008) makes an 'interpretative comment' in order to link the subject matter of his client's drawings to the transference, thus responding to the child's anxiety about the person of the therapist. He reports saying that 'I thought he was wondering about me, whether I was an Eldar with psychic powers, or an inquisitor – how far was I to be trusted?' (Tipple, 2008: 183). Tipple adds that the world portrayed in the child's drawing could reflect his experience of 'boys of his own age'. In the next drawing the child shifts his position in relation to the art therapist. Tipple however uses the word 'translation' for verbal descriptions of images and their contents, as in the example above.

In 2009 Bragge and Fenner describe a model of art therapy practice in which they develop an 'interactive square', a diagrammatic account of interaction between therapist and client in the sessions. This diagram, combined with video recording of the session, affords the opportunity for comparison between actual observable events and the therapist's subjective experience as recorded through process notes. It also offers a visual account of sessions, as an alternative to the more established method of case presentation. They acknowledge the phenomenological roots of their work and they suggest that Skaife argues for 'a more intersubjective approach to make the process more visible and shift the profession from the clutch of psychoanalytic traditions embedded in verbal language and split notions of subject and object' (Bragge and Fenner, 2009: 19).

Rostron (2010) applied Stern's theory of *amodal perception* to the analysis of images made by a 36-year-old man. Her analysis was made retrospectively, a year after work with the client had ended. She says Stern's research into early infancy, based on observation, offered a more phenomenological approach and was consequently more satisfactory than previous attempts at applying Object Relations theory and the Jungian concept of 'active imagination'. She describes a session in which she experienced a mixture of erotic and maternal feelings in response to her client's repetitive fondling of the paint bottles and his use of the materials. 'I often felt drowsy and comfortable when he was painting, my eyelids heavy with a sensation previously experienced during pregnancy and breast feeding' (Rostron, 2010: 41). Her client's repetitive and seductive actions bring to mind Meltzer's advice that there is a need to be active on occasions in order to end repetitive activities (Meltzer *et al.*, 1975).

Since the 'Images and the Emergence of Meaning' conferences at Somerset House in 2000 and 2002, there have been changes in attitude towards the condition of autism itself, and shifts in thinking about the position of the therapist in the context of the therapeutic relationship. There has been a noticeable interest in observable phenomena in the literature about art therapy with people on the autistic spectrum, and a focus on intersubjectivity and the pre-verbal stages of development. This has led to more interactive approaches being incorporated, including the use of art materials themselves.

Neurodiversity

Increased awareness of autism, supported by articulate and distinctive voices from within the autistic community (Temple Grandin and Donna Williams, for example), has contributed towards the emergence of the idea of 'neurodiversity': an acceptance of autism (and other departures from the 'neurotypical') as variations in mental functioning rather than deficits. It is now common to hear the phrase 'autistic spectrum condition' rather than 'autistic spectrum disorder' while those on the spectrum have appropriated and modified the language of the clinician ('aspies', 'autie spectrum'). We can recognise potential areas of strength as well as difficulty in the autist's make-up: originality, honesty, attention to detail and highly focused application to an area of interest. Furthermore, Howard Gardner (1985) has argued for the existence of a number of domains of intelligence, some of which may be more developed in the autistic individual (spatial awareness, for example).

The question becomes one of whether there is something lacking in autistic experience. There is a huge difference between the more assertive proponents of neurodiversity, who deny the need for placing neurological conditions within any remedial or clinical context, and those campaigning to adapt social structures to make more allowance for neural differences (as in autism-friendly film screenings). It is much easier for those at the higher-functioning end of the spectrum to articulate their experiences, and much of the work described in this volume is with individuals whose lives are sorely restricted by autism and associated pervasive learning and social difficulties.

On a related note, there is currently concern that proposed new diagnostic criteria for DSM-V (scheduled for publication in May 2013) will be too stringent, excluding many who would be identified as autistic under the present checklist from treatment and services. The other side of the debate contends that diagnosis has become murky and inexact, with many laying claim to some autistic spectrum characteristics (see, for example, Galan 2012).

The search for an understanding of the aetiology of autism and a possible solution in terms of prevention, rather than cure, is evident in different areas of research, including cognitive science, psychiatry and experimental psychology. The combined findings of these researchers and clinicians make a powerful case against the possibility of autism having a psychogenic origin, a premise that informed earlier psychoanalytic practice with the concomitant implication that the autistic subject could be healed or cured. Most of the authors in this book, despite a vigorous engagement with the struggles that autism can cause individuals, families and services, express a recognition and acceptance of those aspects of the condition that cannot be changed. The focus instead is on qualitative enhancements in (for example) creativity and communication, within the limits of the autist's abilities and personality.

Intersubjectivity

Intersubjectivity is rooted in twentieth century philosophy (Habermas, 1971, in Marshak 1998: 63) and has influenced psychoanalytic thinking about the transference phenomenon in particular. This has effected a change from the emphasis of the psychoanalytic encounter resting on the 'intrapsychic' processes of the patient and the world of their internal objects, to a mutuality between two subjects that recognises 'the difference between experience as perceived outside the self and the subjectively conceived object' (Habermas, in Marshak 1998: 63).

The psychoanalytic definition of intersubjectivity retains an intrapsychic dimension; it is not therefore the same as the interactive or the interpersonal (Habermas, in Marshak 1998: 62). This distinction and the subjectivity of the therapist is not always evident in descriptions of intersubjective approaches to art therapy and may be due to the added dimension and complexity generated through the use of art materials, with the emphasis on the observable process. The therapist's subjectivity may emerge in other ways when, for example, it is realised in her own image-making process and available to her client as a visual statement (see Bragge and Fenner, 2009).

Intersubjectivity has influenced dance movement, music and drama therapy, and has more recently been explored by art therapists through an application of the work of Daniel Stern (1985, 2004). Stern's investigations of the non-verbal communication of infants are akin to the qualities explored by synaesthetes such as Wassily Kandinsky, whose interest in the relationship between musical and colour tones developed into an intricate theory of vibrational correspondences.

Meltzer et al.'s (1975) recommendations for active interventions on the part of the therapist rhyme with several of the authors who describe feeling moved to interact with their client through the art medium (e.g. Jones and 'Elizabeth', Chapter 8, developed an interactive painting game). Some of the authors in this book have said that they would consider working more interactively or have changed their practices to do so. The intersubjective approach might also suggest a more interactive conception of visual arts practice as explored by Bragge and Fenner (2009).

Winnicott (1971a) provided an earlier model of this in his Squiggle game and Fuyoko Takeda describes how this has evolved into the 'drawing conversation' (Takeda, 2011). On occasion, (inter)activity can puncture the hypnagogic atmosphere that sometimes pervades the therapy room in work with people with autism (for example, Jones describes how Elizabeth took action to call her attention).

A partnership between art therapy and psychodynamic theories of early infancy has been well established for many years, particularly in the context of work with children and autism, and it is interesting that Stern's ideas have recently been incorporated so vigorously into this area of art therapy practice. While his theory of early infant development, like other theories before it, can help us to understand the origin of autistic impairments, it focuses more specifically on the 'observed infant'. The emphasis in the literature describing current practice has shifted from seeking to understand unconscious processes in the inner world of the infant to observable, outwardly manifest processes. This is undoubtedly a valuable way of working, as Evans and Dubowski (2001) have demonstrated, though it may also be expedient for us as health practitioners in the current climate of measured outcomes, so that we can be 'seen to be doing something'. Furthermore, an interactive method can alleviate the intense discomfort of working with an unresponsive client (described in many experiences in this book) and it may appeal to us as art therapists because it strengthens the intermediary area we value through the use of our materials.

Although her work is very different from recent art therapy developments described as interactive and intersubjective, Rita Simon's account of her working process provides a vivid example where both the observable *and* intrapsychic aspects of subjectivity can be seen to co-exist:

> I try to follow an experience that is rooted in the unconscious impulses which shape the work: the beginning, when the patient moves to sit or stand before a chosen art material and alters it in some way, through handling of the paint or clay; what is obliterated and what is preserved of the preliminary marks; and the patient's responses to his finished work ... it is this silent dialogue with the art material and the changing emotions that accompany it that is as much if not more important than the final object.
>
> (Simon, 1997)

Transference and countertransference

In the majority of our case studies the authors describe their own subjective states in terms of feelings; for example, feelings of exhaustion and of being excluded. Jones describes 'paralysis, struggle and depletion' and Ashby gives an account of feeling 'wiped out and annihilated'. Most of the authors considered these subjective states to be evidence of a strong countertransference, although Goldsmith refers to her client's 'projections' and Ginsberg refers to 'primitive communications'. In the autistic subjects described, there appears to be a persistence of early infantile states. The reference to 'primitive communications' and 'projection' also points to the Kleinian concept of projective identification, which is an early mode of defence against anxieties engendered, primarily, by the threat of separation.

Bion (1962) extended Klein's concept, recognising that, as well as a defence, projective identification was a means of communication. Through her reverie, the mother (and/or therapist) who serves as a container transforms the infant's raw sense impressions, which are experienced as things-in-themselves, into psychic elements that are then available for thinking about 'through dreaming, imagination and remembering' (Mann, 1989: 11). Mann believes that 'it is possible to extend Bion's concepts to the painting process ... the act of painting, like dreaming, organises sensations and feelings and thus, like the mother, can become an auxiliary ego' (Mann, 1989: 13). We know that imagination is an area of impairment in autism and that the 'central coherence' theory suggests that the act of remembering might be affected by an absence of a sense of continuity. The authors in this book certainly made themselves available through their own reverie but this was not always met, or transformed into an intersubjective state, by their autistic clients.

In Oliver Sacks' account of Temple Grandin, he refers to Grandin's claim that 'she does not have an unconscious [...] she does not repress memories and thoughts, like normal people' (Sacks, 1995: 273). A conception of inner and outer worlds as a structuring principle for experience may be lacking in autism, and there may also not be clear lines of demarcation between subjects, so that it becomes hard to come into relationship. Relating is a process in which symbolic functioning plays a key role in both the interpersonal and intrapsychic realms.

There is another important question raised in Sacks' conversations with Grandin, that of the role of desire. Grandin says she does not have the capacity to 'swoon' or to experience passionate emotional responses, whether in relation to people or in response to music. Desire arises out of a sense of subjectivity and of two subjects in relationship; it asks the question, 'What do you want of me?' (Green, 1990 in Marshak 1998: 62). This is a question that remained unanswered in some of the therapeutic accounts in this book when the therapist is often left feeling unwanted, alienated or 'wiped out'.

Lacan has received little attention from art therapists but his ideas about the imaginary and the symbolic are worth consideration in working with autism. The *imaginary* and the *symbolic* are two of three fundamental orders, the third being the *real*, that form the central principles on which his theories about the human subject are based.

Lacan's account of the imaginary is one of illusion, fascination and seduction (Evans, 1996: 82) and it has its beginnings in the *mirror stage* (see Goldsmith's afterword). The imaginary is the realm of images and appearances and is characterised by duality but it is structured by the symbolic, which is triadic and mediated by a third. The images, ideas and appearances of the imaginary order are merely effects of the symbolic: 'the imaginary exerts a captivating power over the subject, founded in the almost hypnotic effect of the specular image ... the use of the symbolic is the only way to dislodge the disabling fixations of the imaginary' (Evans, 1996: 83).

There are many examples in this book of the seductive quality of our clients' images and the hypnotic effect of repetitive processes in the use of art materials. There is a compelling rationale for the use of interventions and interactive methods to disrupt the possibility of our being drawn into the client's autistic states. However, we must be mindful in our use of interventions when we take an active role in using art materials ourselves; our own art work may also be seductive and mirror an image of perfection that leaves our clients, by comparison, with a fragmented and precarious sense of self, foreclosing on any potential for imaginative activity, however fragile that may be.

Threads and themes

This collection of individual voices and stories alerts us to the emergence of recurring themes in our work with people with autism. Many of these will be familiar to art therapy practitioners but it is the quality of these themes that conveys the particular way in which an autistic spectrum condition can affect the therapeutic relationship.

The use of art materials/processes

There is a broad spectrum in the case material, extending from an anxious over-consumption (Ginsberg) to the complete refusal to make use of materials at all (Dolphin). It is important to note that art making can be used defensively to 'fill up' available time and space, as well as being a vehicle for expression. The use of materials is often very concrete (Ginsberg, Wilson) – paint, paste, water are enjoyed for their physical and sensual properties rather than their symbolic potential. Yet the latter can emerge, even if initially resisted by the autistic client (Moore describes how Simon's images gave him the opportunity to explore his sense of self).

Boundary and space

In a parallel to the use of materials, there may be too much or not enough space, either physically or psychologically. Again the sense is of a difficulty in accessing a shared experience, where understanding, play and communication might occur. Ginsberg reports: 'The reflective space of the session was sucked dry, airless and closed up along with any opportunity for him to allow a sense of "not me"'. Absences and gaps can be hard for autistic people to tolerate (Byers). There may be an unusual or fragile sense of body or self on the part of the client (Goldsmith).

Voicing and silence

Difficulties with communication can affect the course of the therapy considerably, especially when the autistic person also has severe learning difficulties (Ashby). 'Reality testing' – where the therapist verbally test checks her hunches against the client's perceptions – may not be available. Even where there is no developmental delay, silence may characterise the encounter (Dolphin).

The words or silence of the therapist are also important. Even if the specific meaning of commentaries and interpretations is not received, the sound of the words can contribute towards an experience of being met, 'held' or listened to (Byers describes her words as a form of reflecting out loud). But the presence of the therapist, whether they are verbal or silent, can also be experienced as intrusive. In her account of her work with an autistic woman, Goldsmith suggests that her client's portrayal of her had associations with a drawing depicting an 'angry voice'.

Images, imagination and symbols

The term 'image' has been applied broadly in this book to include, verbal, visual, perceptual and mental images. Art therapy involves the use of all four in a process of intertwining and exchange.

Sometimes when there is silence in the session accompanied by an absence of symbolic or imaginative activity from the client, the therapist's own mental imagery can facilitate an understanding or a symbolic representation that the client finds hard to do for him or herself. Often aspects of the therapeutic relationship, affective climate or countertransference are striking: for instance, in Dolphin's image of a small animal frozen in headlights.

An absence of a symbolic attitude is described by Wilson in her account of Chris, who worked through an immediate relationship with the paint, commenting on what he was doing and on the changing identity of the images. When he cut into one of his pictures with scissors, he feared damage to the actual person he was depicting.

Jones recounts how Elizabeth obscured her conventionally readable face schemas under layers of paint, indicating that she may have been using the therapy for a regression to earlier, less differentiated states of mind. However, regression is not always evident in work with autists in light of the developmental delay component of the condition.

The process of representation may strike us as unusual, as in the case of Moore's client, Simon, when he is painting a cake in a way that seems to be enacting and repeating a process of taking a slice from the cake but not eating it. This illustrates how there is often rich symbolic potential if not symbolic intent.

Art therapy and the autistic client

The expressive arts therapies – music therapy, dance movement therapy, dramatherapy and art therapy – are particularly well placed to work in the autist's likely areas of difficulty. Though by no means exclusive to these disciplines, they do highlight the use of playful interaction and imagination.

As we saw in the introduction, personal relationships may not provide an experience of safety and containment for people with autism (particularly relationships beyond the attachment to the primary caregiver). Rituals and structures take the place of relational bonds. Art is a kind of ordering activity, but one that offers the potential for flexible exploration, spontaneity, play and discovery, sometimes in an interactive context.

Aesthetic activity ('aesthetic' comes from the Greek *aisthanesthai*, to feel or perceive) can allow for more diffuse emotional experiences and expressions than raw face-to-face encounters and communications. In the visual arts especially, there is the possibility of joint attention on a shared task without the 'glare' of a direct exchange; examples in this book include the client and therapist looking at photos together (Dolphin), or looking at each other through the medium of a reflecting pool of coloured water (Jones). The triangulation furnished by the therapist–art work–client relationship can mediate intimacy, which may otherwise be overwhelming for an autistic person.

Art making provides a way for client and therapist to be together, to create a visual record of the experience, and it offers the potential for a relational exchange. The client may also use artistic activity to regulate the amount of interpersonal closeness. We see this for instance in the very self-contained mark making employed by Colin in Ashby's account which the practitioner experiences as frustrating, controlling and excluding.

The predominance of visual thinking in many autistic individuals indicates the particular relevance of art therapy. Julia Kellerman's (2001) description of the special resonance of 'pre-attentive vision' was referred to previously. Kellerman cites Temple Grandin as an autistic person whose thinking, while it may be limited to the visual mode, is characterised by extraordinary detail. Many approaches to autism in the field of special education are centred around visual supports; for example, PECS (Picture Exchange Communication System), in which the student requests a desired item by giving a pictogram to a communication partner, and Comic Strip Conversations, simple visual representations of the possible levels of communication in a social exchange (Gray, 1994).

As Wing's triad acknowledges, autism is characterised by an 'unusual quality' rather than an absence of imagination. Unencumbered by an exclusive focus on one (conventional) perspective, the autist may be able to see and represent things in new and surprising ways. We see a suggestion of this in Moore's description of the images made by Simon, which often feature strange and interesting viewpoints.

Video recording

The use of video to record sessions is a strategy being considered by art therapists, and is a method employed regularly by music therapists working with learning disabled clients. Video can be a means of assessment, of gathering and presenting evidence and of reflection. Like clinical supervision, it provides a potential triangulating experience, a different viewpoint that might reveal things the therapist has missed or ways in which client responses were slightly different from how they were experienced or remembered. It can be an especially useful tool when development is very slow or very subtle (as in Ashby's account of Colin).

There are losses as well as gains bound up with the use of video. The 'triangulation' is enacted in the manifest world and goes outside the session rather than remaining a symbolic process within the session. That said, the symbolic, as a process facilitated by the therapist in the session, may be problematic when working with people with autism and learning disabilities where subjective exchanges are less frequent. The use of video may well compensate for an absence of any symbolic space between therapist and client by disrupting the imaginary dual nature of the therapeutic encounter and mediating a third area.

Augmenting the traditional art therapy approach: new thinking, new theories

Working in the area of difficulty

At the start of the book we noted that autism is manifest as a triad of impairments in a subject's capacity for communication, imagination and social interaction – those very areas, in fact, on which the success of art therapy depends. So is psychodynamic art therapy with the autistic person a doomed enterprise? There is an opposite argument: that there is no learning or development without work taking place in the client's area of deficit or difficulty.

In arguing for the effectiveness of psychoanalytic psychotherapy with this client group, Urwin (2011) first points out – as we noted in our introduction – that individuals with autism do not necessarily lack affect; indeed, they can be highly sensitive to shifts in the emotional atmosphere around them. They may, however, need support to organise and regulate their affective lives. Approaching this goal demands 'the psychotherapist's preparedness to be affected emotionally by the child's behaviour and voluntary or involuntary communications, to work in the transference' (Urwin, 2011: 259).

Urwin highlights the need for adjustments to both therapeutic technique and the practitioner's hopes for treatment. For example, the therapist does not expect the development of empathy, but rather hopes for an enhanced ability on the part of the client to recognise and connect with his own emotional state. Correspondingly, interpretations are focused on describing the affective qualities that prevail in the session, rather than uncovering the client's unconscious attitudes towards the therapist. Another form of intervention is to provide alternative perspectives (rather than insights), encouraging tolerance (rather than understanding) of a 'third position' (Urwin, 2011: 258).

Winnicott's 'potential space' (1971b) happens when the infant begins to realise that there is another being, his mother. Connected with both external reality and the child's inner experiences and sensations, the potential space is distinct from either. It occurs between him and his mother and is a third area where the infant plays. Russian psychologist Lev Vygotsky described a zone of proximal development (ZPD), which is an 'area' beyond what is known, in which something new can be learnt. Beyond this zone new information cannot yet be learnt because it is too different from what is known. Art therapy can provide an area between the therapist and client that can be both a potential space and a zone of proximal development. Like Winnicott, Vygotsky stressed the importance of play as a lynchpin of development. Sensitively focused challenges within the ZPD or potential space can support aptitudes that are on the threshold of emergence; for the autistic client, these might include new interpersonal skills, an increased capacity to play or a move towards symbolic expression. Art therapy and related psychotherapeutic disciplines provide a safer, more contained practice arena than everyday forms of social interaction. Moreover, the regularity of session times with consistent boundaries and structure can be valuable for people with autism, offering a predictable frame within which there is the potential for them to make and master manageable variations in their repertoire.

Client-centred and holistic approaches in special education

Our core art therapy stance – using a person's (inter)actions, personality, affective state, strengths and needs to shape the content of the sessions – now also informs approaches in social care and special education. Dave Hewett and Melanie Nind, working with people with severe learning disabilities at Harperbury Hospital, developed an approach to non-verbal communication known as 'Intensive Interaction' (Nind and Hewett, 1994). Intensive Interaction aims to teach the 'fundamentals of communication' – for example, shared attention, taking turns, understanding eye contacts – through strategies such as responding to (mirroring or re-casting) vocalisations and joint play. These areas of work are very relevant to many people with autism.

Hewett argues that acquiring the fundamentals of communication is the most complicated learning anyone can do, and that it is presumptuous, even a kind of philistinism, to try to facilitate this kind of learning through rigid pre-planning. In fact – and again we find echoes of Vygotsky and Winnicott – play is by far the most suitable approach. This thinking chimes with the more fluid, open structures described in the accounts of art therapy practice gathered in this book.

Hewett's more recent work also points up the central role of 'phatic' communication (Hewett, 2011: 9–13). Phatic communications are those whose aim is not primarily functional, for example to ask for something or to give instructions. Instead their primary aim is to foster social bonding and emotional contact, 'the hot air of companionship' (Hewett, 2011: 9). Hewett proposes that 65 per cent of human communication falls into this category. Yet the majority of clinical and educational interventions in the learning disability field (and this includes many people on the autism spectrum) address the remaining 35 per cent – that is, communication skills with a specific, concrete outcome. Art therapy is well placed to contribute towards a necessary counterbalance in services, providing an arena for social, affective and creative exchanges with more open and fluid goals. This is relevant to 'higher-functioning' autistic individuals as well as those who communicate mainly non-verbally.

Mentalisation

Joint attention is a fundamental component of a 'theory of mind' and the allied skill of 'mentalisation', the ability to recognise the mental states of self and others that underlie outward behaviour. Mentalisation-based approaches are being actively explored by art therapists. Neil Springham (2012) outlines the key principles of the model, including an open and transparent questioning of the client's understanding of the motives of others and an avoidance of metaphor when the ability to mentalise is reduced. These two parameters are clearly relevant to work with autistic people. Springham also stresses the danger of an over-emphasis on feeling at the expense of thinking and reflection, and advocates the use of interpretation as a means of highlighting alternative perspectives rather than the promotion of insight.

Some of the art therapy described in the current volume, although not intentionally using a mentalisation approach (a relatively recent addition to the clinical repertoire), shows the potential of art making to open a space for thinking and reflection in the context of a charged encounter (for example, drawing Margaret while she was asleep opened up Goldsmith's thinking about her client).

Cognitive components

There may be a role for cognitive elements in art therapy practice. Though we should be wary of assuming that changes in a client's artistic expression (for example, a move towards representation) necessarily go hand in hand with developmental gains, the therapist can supply different visual paradigms; as, for example, in Bragge and Fenner's use of the 'interactive square' (2009). This more active approach can also convey the idea that the practitioner is an independent other, a generator of his or her own thoughts and representations. Therapeutic reflections and responses contain modifications, creating an analogue rather than a reproduction of the client's original material.

Moreover, there is an overlap between the spheres of cognition and affectivity, and movements in each may be mutually influential. The field of 'Interpersonal Neurobiology', developed by Allan Schore and Dan Siegel, posits that interpersonal/therapeutic encounters can promote neural flexibility, physically opening up new pathways (Siegel, 2010).

Joined-up working

A vital component of the psychotherapeutic enterprise portrayed by Urwin (2011) is the involvement of families and schools. This ensures that parents (for example) have realistic hopes and expectations for treatment. In some cases, examples of change provided by the therapist help family members reflect upon their child's nascent abilities. Without robust collaboration, therapeutic gains can be vulnerable to a lack of continuity or effective follow up (witness the impact of a poorly managed school transition on Elizabeth in Jones' case study). It is important for art therapists to be able to contribute their knowledge and understanding within multi-disciplinary teams in order to promote 'joined-up' service provision. And importantly, positive reports from families and schools contribute to the body of evidence supporting the effectiveness of treatment.

Neuropsychoanalysis

The field of neuropsychoanalysis, established as a distinct discipline just before the turn of the millennium, aims to bring together psychoanalysis, psychoanalytic theory and neuroscientific discovery. This is a rich source for art therapists and for those working in the field of autism, with the potential to generate new ways of thinking about autistic conditions and the role and function of art therapy. Mark Solms' paper, 'The Conscious Id' (Solms, 2011), vindicates much classical Freudian thinking and theory, while also pointing out errors in Freud's models of the mind. Solms maps out two distinct areas of the organ of the mind – the primary brain stem and the secondary cortical 'grey matter'. Making a radical case for the consciousness of what Freud called *The Id*, and showing its location in the organs of the brain stem, Solms argues that this is the site of primary process. He goes on to explain vividly how the cortex evolved to constrain and sculpt primary affect and transform it into cognition. Thus, the free energy of the conscious Id is moulded and bound by the unconscious Ego as we learn from experience.

Woven through the theories of autism presented in this volume runs a theme of disjunction: we have seen that Kanner (1943) described the autist as being unable to relate himself in the ordinary way to people and situations. Asperger (1944) observed a disembodied quality and a disjuncture between affect and intellect. Frith (1989) referred to perception and cognition being atomised so that the autist remains lost in a welter of detail, while Baron-Cohen *et al.* (1985) talk in terms of an absence of theory of mind meaning that relationships are not experienced as containing. Meltzer *et al.* (1975) refer to an absence of psychic coherence leaving the individual lost in unthinking reverie. Tustin (1981) posited encapsulated and confusional types, while Ogden (1989) says that pathological autism involves unbounded sensation not eased by learning from experience. Stern (1985) posits the observed and the clinical infant, while Habermas (1971, in Marshak 1998) differentiates between experience as perceived outside the self and the subjectively conceived object. And Grandin (Sacks, 1995) asserts that she doesn't have an unconscious, saying that for her 'nothing is hidden ... In me, the amygdala doesn't generate enough emotion to lock the files of the hippocampus' (Sacks, 1995: 273).

All of these ways of conceptualising the autistic condition rhyme with Solms' radical concept of the primary consciousness of the brain stem that finds expression through the secondary and unconscious functions of the cortex; those functions that give us our (unreliable) impressions of our own bodies, our environment and our relationships. Could it be that in the autistic individual, communication between brain stem and cortex is disrupted, leaving the individual either flooded with 'raw data' or else, as Grandin puts it, 'without enough emotion' to activate certain processes in the mind? This has to remain an open question at this stage, but in relation to our work as art therapists, we can think about which part of a person's mind we are trying to reach through our work. Are we aiming to stimulate neural activity or even growth in a particular area of the cortical brain, as in the interpersonal neurobiology of Schore and Siegel (Siegel, 2010)? Are we trying to reach the area of underlying instinctual, affective consciousness detailed by psychoanalyst Solms? Or can we integrate work in both registers, so that the analytic can breathe life into the biological, just as Stern's (1985) clinical infant breathes subjective life into the observed infant?

Conclusion

Although our case studies have highlighted the need for endurance and persistence, the writers have not sustained the work through faith alone. There are positive outcomes; for example Elizabeth's tentative journey towards symbolic expression (Jones), Peter's enhanced ability to face the unpredictable world outside his sessions (Ginsberg) and Colin's requests for art materials to help him manage his feelings (Ashby). The issue is not the absence of progress, but whether that progress is robust and sustainable.

Art therapists have to engage with the contemporary call for evidence-based practice where randomised controlled trials are currently held up as the arbiter of 'best practice'. This seems like an impossible task if we are to continue to practise in individual ways with such a small population. Nevertheless, our case work itself constitutes rich qualitative 'material', where the challenge lies in how we can analyse and present it. Rostron (2010) for instance, describes a method of analysing art therapy retrospectively. Theory is a living field, continually emerging from the observations and hypotheses of researchers and practitioners, building upon and challenging previous thinking. Knowledge is not 'achieved', but is constantly in a state of evolution, so as practitioners we can be open to playing and experimenting with new ideas as well as ingesting and applying pre-existing concepts.

Art therapy remains one of the main modalities through which a psychodynamic encounter can be made available to people with autism, particularly when the person is also affected by profound and complex learning disabilities. The methods and approaches surveyed in this closing chapter can provide starting points and, in some cases, a way to work more interactively; or, as Anne Alvarez has it, to remain in 'live company' (Alvarez, 1992). Theory and imagination supply us with structures for thinking and a means to sustain our engagement; but, in the final analysis, when the therapist is in a room with another person (or people), she often falls back on raw psychic resources in finding a way to *be* with the other(s). Sometimes, the practitioner's intuitions will anticipate elements of future practice.

If we stay with the process and tolerate the uncertainty that it entails, it can produce a full and rich encounter that leads to changes in both therapist and client. Presenting some of our encounters here, in the form of case studies, is a way of sharing lived experience so that the impact of a therapeutic intervention on an individual basis can be evaluated.

References

Alvarez, A. (1992) *Live Company: Psychoanalytic Psychotherapy with Autistic, Borderline, Deprived and Abused Children*, London: Routledge.
Asperger, H. (1944) 'Die Autistischen Psychopathen im Kindesalter', *Archiv fur Psychiatrie und Nervenkrakheiten*, 177: 76–136.
Baron-Cohen, S., Alan, L. and Frith, U. (1985) 'Does the autistic child have a "theory of mind"?', *Cognition*, 21 (1): 37–46.
Barrett, L. and Dorko, P.T. (2012) 'The Piano Lesson'. Online. Available at: www.barrettdorko.com/articles/piano.htm (accessed 27 October 2012).
Bion, W.R. (1962) *Learning from Experience*, London: Karnac.
Bragge, A. and Fenner, P. (2009) 'The emergence of the "interactive square" as an approach to art therapy with children on the autistic spectrum', *International Journal of Art Therapy*, 14 (1): 17–28.
Evans, D. (1996) *An Introductory Dictionary of Lacanian Analysis*, London: Routledge.
—— (2005) *An Introductory Dictionary of Lacanian Analysis*, London and New York: Routledge.
Evans, K. and Dubowski, J. (2001) *Art Therapy with Children on the Autistic Spectrum: Beyond Words*, London and Philadelphia: Jessica Kingsley Publishers Ltd.
Frith, U. (1989) *Autism: Explaining the Enigma*, Oxford: Blackwell.
Galan, C. (2012) 'Proposed DSM-V criteria for autism sparks debate'. Online. Available at: http://beta.in-mind.org/social-psychology-headlines/proposed-dsm-v-criteria-autism-sparks-debate (accessed 20 October 2012).
Gardner, H. (1985) *Frames of the Mind: The Theory of Multiple Intelligences*, London: Paladin.
Gray, C. (1994) *Comic Strip Conversations: Colourful, Illustrated Interactions with Students with Autism and Related Disorders*, Michigan: Jenison Public Schools.
Henley, D. (2001) 'Annihilation anxiety and fantasy in the art of children with Asperger's Syndrome and others on the autistic spectrum', *American Journal of Art Therapy*, 39 (4): 113–21.

Hewett, D. (2011) 'Intensive Interaction and Challenging Behaviour'. Online. Available at: www.ldiag.org.uk/documents/DaveHewettIntensiveInteraction.pdf (accessed 26 October 2012).

Kanner, L. (1943) 'Autistic disturbances of affective contact', *Nervous Child*, 2: 217–50.

Kellerman, J. (2001) *Autism, Art and Children: The Stories we Draw*, Westport, CT and London: Bergin and Garvey.

Klein, M. (1975) *Envy and Gratitude and Other Works 1946–1963*, London: Hogarth.

Laplanche, J. and Pontalis, J.B. (1973) *The Language of Psychoanalysis*, London: Karnac.

Mann, D. (1989) 'The talisman or projective identification? A critique', *Inscape: The Journal of the British Association of Art Therapists*, autumn: 11–15.

Marshak, M.D. (1998) 'The intersubjective nature of analysis' in Allister, I. and Hauke, C. (eds), *Contemporary Jungian Analysis*, London and New York: Routledge.

Meltzer, D., Bremner, J., Hoxter, S., Weddell, D. and Wittenberg, I. (1975) *Explorations in Autism: A Psychoanalytic Study*, Strath Tay: Clunie Press.

Meyerowitz-Katz, J. (2008) ' "Other people have a secret that I do not know": art psychotherapy in private practice with an adolescent girl with Asperger's syndrome' in Case, C. and Dalley, T. (eds), *Art Therapy with Children from Infancy to Adolescence*, London and New York: Routledge.

Nind, M. and Hewett, D. (1994) *Access to Communication*, London: David Fulton.

Ogden, T. (1989, reprinted edition 1992) *The Primitive Edge of Experience*, London: Karnac.

Patterson, Z. (2008) 'From "beanie" to "Boy" ' in Case, C. and Dalley, T. (eds), *Art Therapy with Children from Infancy to Adolescence*', London and New York: Routledge.

Rostron, J. (2010) 'On amodal perception and language in art therapy with autism', *International Journal of Art Therapy*, 15: 136–49.

Sacks, O. (1995) *An Anthropologist on Mars*, London: Picador.

Siegel, D. (2010) 'More About Interpersonal Neurobiology'. Online. Available at: http://drdansiegel.com/about/interpersonal_neurobiology/ (accessed 17 October 2011).

Simon, R. (1997) *Symbolic Images in Art Therapy*, London and New York: Routledge.

Skaife, S. (2001) 'Making visible: art therapy and intersubjectivity', *Journal of the British Association of Art Therapists*, 6 (2): 40–50.

Solms, M. (2011) 'The conscious Id', New York Lecture, Neuropsa. Online. Available at: www.neuropsa.org.uk (accessed 8 January 2012).

Springham, N. (2012) 'How Can the Arts Help People to Think?' British Association of Art Therapists. Online. Available at: www.baat.org/Neil_Springham_slides2.pdf (accessed 27 October 2012).

Stern, D. (1985) *The Interpersonal World of the Infant: A View from Psychoanalysis and Developmental Psychology*, New York: Basic Books.

—— (2004) *The Present Moment in Psychotherapy and Everyday Life*, New York: W.W. Norton & Co., Inc.

Takeda, F. (2011) 'Express Intent', *SEN Magazine Online*. Available at: www.senmagazine.co.uk/articles/393-how-can-art-therapy-help-children-with-learning-difficulties-to-understand-and-communicate-their-feelings.html (accessed 29 October 2012).

—— (1994) 'Communication and interpretation in art therapy with people who have a learning disability', *Inscape: The Journal of the British Association of Art Therapists*, 2: 31–5.

Tipple, R. (2008) 'Paranoia and paracosms: brief art therapy with a youngster with Asperger's Syndrome', in Case, C. and Dalley, T. (eds), *Art Therapy with Children from Infancy to Adolescence*, London and New York: Routledge.

Tustin, F. (1981, revised edition 1992) *Autistic States in Children*, London and New York: Routledge.

Urwin, C. (2011) 'Emotional life of autistic spectrum children: what do we want from child psychotherapy treatment?' *Psychoanalytic Psychotherapy*, 25 (3): 245–61.

Vygotsky, L.S. (1934) *Interaction Between Learning and Development*, translated by M. Lopez-Morillas, reprinted in Cole, M., John-Steiner, V., Scribner, S. and Souberman, E. (eds) (1978), *Mind in Society: The Development of Higher Psychological Processes*, Cambridge, MA: Harvard, pp. 79–91.

Winnicott, D. (1971a) *Therapeutic Consultations in Child Psychiatry*, London: Hogarth & IPA.

—— (1971b) *Playing and Reality*, London: Tavistock.

Index

academia 85
active imagination 86, 134
adaptation xi, 31, 67, 73, 76, 79, 81–2, 135
adolescence 17—18, 22, 33, 119–20, 130, 148–9
aesthetic 1, 5, 17, 105, 107, 141
affect(ive) 2, 4, 7–8, 15, 16–17, 19, 32–3, 77, 79, 83–4, 86, 105, 107, 110, 115–17, 131, 140, 142–6
affection 90, 92–3, 113
aggression 92–3
Alister, I. 85, 87
alternative script 20
Alvarez, A. 5, 16, 41, 48–50, 105, 108, 118, 147
ambivalence 11, 27–8, 125
amodal perception 17, 74, 103, 131, 134, 148
anal 52
anguish 30
anxiety 9, 11, 17, 22, 24, 29–30, 37–8, 42, 86, 129, 133–4, 147
annihilation 9, 17, 133, 147
archetypal 26, 86–8
artefact 75–6, 112
art making 19, 31, 35, 73, 129, 139, 141, 144
art materials 5, 7–8, 13–14, 23–24, 26, 35–6, 39, 42, 45–9, 51, 55–6, 62, 67, 72–3, 75–6, 79–82, 84, 86, 94, 98–99, 106, 110, 115, 122, 128–9, 133–6, 139, 146
art work 7, 9, 15, 19, 23, 26, 31–2, 36, 55, 60–1, 96–7, 99–100, 105, 112, 115, 123–4, 128, 139, 141
Ashby, E. 102
as if 84
Asperger, H. 2–3, 16, 20, 145, 147
Asperger's Syndrome (AS) 3, 13, 16–21, 23–4, 26, 31–33, 130–1, 133, 147–9
assessment 3, 13, 19, 22, 26–7, 30, 32, 38, 50, 73, 106–7, 109, 118, 121, 124, 130, 142
attachment theory 86–7
attitude of availability 105
attunement 25, 63, 73–4
Attwood, A. 3, 16–18, 20, 23, 26–7, 32
autistic contiguous position 14, 65–6, 69–70, 73
autistic continuum 3, 20, 24, 30
autistic object 72–3, 84
autistic sensation objects 66
autistic spectrum i, iii, xi, 1, 3–4, 10, 12–13, 16–17, 24, 26, 28, 31–2, 46, 63, 73–4, 89, 102, 119–20, 133, 135, 139, 144, 147, 149
autistic traits 76, 90, 100, 119, 129

baby 9, 25, 39, 41–2, 57, 66–7, 100, 113, 118, 121, 126

Index

Balint, M. 115, 117, 118
Baron-Cohen, S. 4, 16, 145, 147
Barrett, L. & Dorko, P.T. 147
bereavement 13, 26, 30, 43, 131
Bettelheim, B. 9, 16
Bick, E. 10, 41, 49
Bion, W. 10, 14, 16, 46, 49, 65–6,73–4, 105, 138, 147
bite 54, 106, 123, 125; biting 67
black hole 37, 108
bodily separateness 9, 29, 12
body 10, 15, 23, 29, 47, 52–3, 65–6, 70, 72–3, 76, 78–9, 86, 90, 110, 112, 121–2, 125, 139; body language 23, 52, 78, 90; disembodied 2, 78, 84, 125, 145
boundary, boundaries 7–8, 14, 46–7, 72, 76, 78, 90, 92–4, 97, 99, 101, 124, 139, 143
boundedness 66; *unboundedness* 70
Bragge & Fenner 16, 31–2, 73–4, 96, 102, 134, 136, 144, 147
brain 73, 106, 133, 145–6; brain stem 106, 145–6
breaks 14, 38, 106, 111, 113
breathing 25
Bromfield, R. 130
brother 38, 54, 60, 106, 127
Bungener, J. & McCormack, B. 120, 131

CAMHS 106
Case, C. 11, 16–18, 33, 38, 49, 148–9
cellophane 8, 76, 84
Central Coherence Theory 3–4, 9, 85, 138
chaos 20, 57–8, 62, 92
challenging behaviour 21, 89, 99, 101–2, 148
circles 68, 70, 91–2, 95, 106
clay 52, 58–9, 137
client-centred 94, 143
clinical infant 12, 146

cognitive i, 2–3, 18–19, 29, 37–8, 65, 85, 105, 120, 136, 144
Cohn, H. 27, 30, 33
collude, collusion 13, 24, 27, 36, 84
Comic Strip Conversations 141, 147
commissioning 32
community x, 51, 135; community nurse 21–2, 28–30
collaborative 89–90, 94, 96, 98–102, 130
complexes 85–6
complexity 87, 136
concrete 4, 8, 11, 23–4, 29, 31, 72, 139, 144
confusion 24, 30, 39, 79, 85, 92
confusional child 9, 145
conscious 6, 25, 42, 53, 67, 72, 78, 86, 118, 145–6, 148
Conscious Id 118, 145, 148
container-contained 66–7, 69, 73
containment 14, 35–6, 40–2, 48, 65, 69, 73, 90, 92, 98, 100, 134, 141
Contemporary Independents 10
continuity 8–10, 14, 62, 66, 101, 138, 145
control 6, 15, 19, 22–3, 30–1, 45, 49, 58, 66, 69–70, 84, 89, 95, 141
cornflour 39–42
countertransference 5–7, 17, 19–20, 25, 32, 36, 70, 90, 93–4, 99, 101, 115, 137, 140
creativity 5, 23, 31, 53, 62, 89, 99–101, 118, 136
Cundall, A. 20, 23, 33
cut up 57

Dalley, T. 11, 16–18, 33, 37, 49, 131, 148–9
deadened 19, 24, 66, 109–10
death 21, 24, 26, 28, 30, 43
defence 5, 9, 11, 17, 20, 25, 33, 62, 66, 82, 85, 87, 103, 116–18, 129, 131, 138; defensive 30, 52, 82, 84, 116, 139

de-integration 81
depressed 55, 57, 121; depression 20, 27
depressive position 11, 65
desire xiii, 2, 4, 13, 23–4, 27, 31, 36, 39–40, 49, 96, 118, 126, 138
de-skilled 6, 79, 86, 90, 101
destroy 25, 57–8, 67, 92, 109
development(al) xiii, 2, 4–5, 8–19, 25, 36–40, 46, 50–3, 57–9, 62, 65, 67, 75–6, 79, 81–2, 86–7, 96–7, 99, 101, 103, 105, 113, 115–121, 129, 133, 135, 137, 140, 142–4, 148–9; developmental stages 11, 19, 53, 99, 119–20
diagnosis xi, 3, 15, 17–18, 21, 26–7, 33, 55, 76, 119–20, 135
diagrammatic 78, 134
dialogue 96, 115, 123, 137
directive 31, 49, 62; non-directive 5, 7, 62–3, 94, 117
dissociation 86
distress 37, 54, 76, 78–9, 96
drama therapist 89, 94, 101–2, 136, 141
drawing conversation 137
dread 13, 38, 41
DSM-III 2, 16
DSM -IV 16, 18–19, 32
DSM-V 16, 135, 147
Dubowski, J. 16, 73–4, 133, 137, 147

ECT 76
Edwards, D. 18–19, 33
ego 8, 10–11, 13, 17, 81–2, 84–6, 138, 145; *ego complex* 85–6
embodied 85
emergent self 45, 115
empathy 4, 20–1, 31, 130, 142
empirical xi, 4, 86
emptiness 13, 23, 35–7, 42, 46, 48–9
encapsulated 66, 68, 70, 72, 86, 94, 117, 145; encapsulation 24, 30, 73
encapsulated child 9, 145

envy 32, 96, 148
epilepsy 89
erotic 134
Evans, D. 138–9, 147
Evans, K. 12, 16, 23, 25, 28, 33, 39, 50, 73–4, 86–7, 105, 133, 137, 147
evidence-based practice ix, xi, 32, 146
excitement 58, 68, 92
experientially 72, 115
exploring 14, 29, 51, 58, 124
expression 2–4, 7, 15, 23, 25, 36, 42–3, 62, 68, 111, 122–3, 129, 139, 141, 143–4, 146
external world 37, 80
eye contact 23, 25, 55, 76, 110, 112–13, 143

face 20, 25, 30, 43–7, 54, 57, 59, 61, 66, 78, 100, 108–12, 117, 122, 127–8, 140
fantasy 17, 85, 133, 147
Farhi, N. 105, 118
father 21–2, 25–6, 28, 30, 38, 54, 96, 99, 106, 121, 127
fear(s) 11, 22, 25, 28, 37, 42, 46, 52, 66, 70, 76, 98, 122–3, 125–6, 129–30, 140
feeding 24, 41, 66–7, 81, 120, 125–6, 135
figurative 23, 60
finger paint 57–8
flow(ing) 14, 40, 42, 65, 68–70, 72–3
food 15, 79, 121, 125–7
Fordham, M. 13, 76, 81–2, 87
Fox, L. 12, 16, 21, 24, 29, 33, 46, 50, 99–100, 102, 119, 131
Freud, A. 105
Freud, S. 6–7, 13, 86, 145
Frith, U. 3–4, 16, 75, 81, 85, 87, 145, 147
frozen 19, 22, 125, 140

frustration 20, 26, 38, 53, 67–8, 90, 94, 99, 101, 126
fury 70
fusing 23

Gafni, S. 101–2
Galan, C. 16, 135, 147
gap 13–14, 37–9, 41–3, 54, 71–2, 75, 107, 126, 139
Gardner, H. 16, 135, 147
gaze 57, 59, 76, 100, 112
Gentle Teaching 89, 102
Gould, J. 3, 18
Graham, W. S. xiii, 35, 50
Grandin, T. 17, 135, 138, 141, 146
Gray, C. 141, 147
grieving 19, 26
group dynamics 52

Habermas 136, 146
hardness 70, 72
Halliday, D. 76, 87
Happé, F. 85, 87
Harperbury Hospital 143
Henley, D. 17, 133, 147
Hewett, D. 89, 102, 143–4, 148
Hoffman, S. 101–2
holding 8, 13–14, 17, 39, 41, 46, 65–6, 69, 73–4
hole 67
Hughes, R. 131

Id 13, 118, 145, 148
identity xii, 8, 13, 29, 51, 75–6, 79, 124, 140
image xiii, 7–8, 10, 12, 17, 19, 21, 22–3, 26, 30–1, 43, 45–7, 49, 60, 66–7, 75–6, 78, 82, 86, 88, 93–6, 98, 100, 112–13, 115, 117–18, 120, 122–7, 129, 133–5, 138–141, 148
image-making 14, 23, 26, 31, 83–4, 92, 97–9, 101, 119, 129, 136

'Images and the Emergence of Meaning' conferences xi, 1, 135
Imaginary, the 75, 86, 138–9; *imaginary order* 86, 138
imagination 1, 10, 14, 28, 75–6, 79, 86, 119, 138, 140–2, 147
impingement 41, 67, 116, 125
incontinent 53, 57
individuation 81
inner world 10, 20, 80, 137
insulin coma 76
interaction 2–5, 7–8, 12, 24, 48–9, 52, 56, 68, 73, 81–2, 85, 89, 97, 99, 102, 113, 118, 133–4, 141–3, 147–9; *Intensive Interaction* 89, 102, 143, 148
interactive art therapy 133
interactive square 16, 31–2, 74, 96, 102, 134, 144, 147
internal space 66
internal working model 87
internalise 66–7
interpenetrating mix-up 115
interpersonal 1–2, 8, 14, 17, 32, 50, 74, 87, 118, 136, 138, 141, 143–6, 148; *interpersonal neurobiology* 144, 146, 148
interpretation 10–12, 18, 23, 72, 84–5, 118, 131, 133–4, 140, 142, 144, 148
interpretative comment 134
intersubjective/intersubjectivity 6, 17, 32, 73, 89, 115–17, 134–8, 148
intrapsychic 136–8
intrusive 20, 25, 69, 81, 84, 92–3, 113, 140; non-intrusive 92
intuition 27, 32, 147
isolated 2, 9, 52, 56, 121
I Spy 77–8, 83–5

Jacobs, M. xiii, 105, 115, 118
joined up 145
jokes 57

Jones, R.E. 116, 118
Jung, C. 6, 8, 10, 13–14, 17, 75–6, 81, 85–8, 134, 148; post-Jungian 14, 75, 85

Kandinsky, W. 136
Kanner, L. 2, 8, 119, 126, 145
Karkou, V. 37, 50
Kellerman, J. 17, 133, 141, 148
kinaesthetic experience 23
Klauber, T. 37, 50
Klein, M. 8, 10–12, 17, 65, 125–6, 131, 138, 148; post-Kleinian 5, 10, 16
Klin, A. 21, 14, 33
Knox, J. 86–8
Kuczaj, E. 131

Lacan, J. 10, 86–7, 138, 147
Laplanche, J. & Pontalis, J.B. 6, 17, 148
latent 10, 79
leaking 66, 73
Leslie, A. 4, 16
live company 118, 147
loss 9, 11, 19, 21–2, 24–5, 30, 42–3, 68, 84–5, 98, 101, 113, 126, 129, 131, 142

MacLagen, D. 11, 17
Mahler, M. 12
Makaton 54
Mann, D. 138, 148
Marshak, M. D. 136, 138, 146, 148
maternal object 9, 42, 46, 118
McCormack, B. 22, 120, 131
McGee, J. 89, 102
meaning(ful) 4, 6, 8, 10–11, 16, 22, 25, 33, 43, 67, 73, 75–6, 79, 84–6, 92, 105–9, 111–13, 115, 124, 128–9, 135, 140, 145
medication 59, 98
Meltzer, D. 9, 17, 135–6, 145, 148
mentalisation 32, 144

merger 81
mess 58, 62, 70, 92, 97, 117
metaphor 4, 11, 68, 85, 105, 108, 113, 116, 127, 144
Meyerowitz-Katz, J. 17, 134, 148
mindful 7, 109, 139
Milner, M. 105, 118
mind 4–5, 7, 16, 22, 24–5, 29, 32, 41–2, 57, 66, 69–70, 72–3, 79, 83, 86–8, 94, 106, 108–9, 112, 115, 117, 120–2, 124–6, 133–5, 140, 145–7; mindless 47; hold/keep in mind 38, 42, 129; *theory of mind* 4, 16, 20, 144–5, 147
mirroring 57, 63, 100, 143
mirror stage 86, 138
Mitchell, J. 126, 131
music therapy/therapist 15, 21, 27, 89, 94, 102, 141–2
moderate learning difficulties 13, 15, 37, 105
mother 9, 21–2, 25, 30, 36, 38, 41–2, 57, 59, 65–7, 73, 78–9, 81–2, 84, 99–100, 103, 113, 118, 120–2, 125–7, 130, 138, 143
mutism 20, 106

neglect 61, 90
neurobiology 144, 146, 148
neurodiversity 1, 135
neurophysiological 30
Newham, P. 25, 33
neuropsychoanalysis 117, 145
night terrors 121
nothingness 38, 42, 66
not being 108
not knowing 36
nourish(ing) 79, 109, 123, 125

object relations 10, 12, 49, 115, 126, 134
observable phenomena xi, 134, 135–7
observed infant 12, 137, 146

occupational therapist 100
Oedipal 96
Ogden, T. 9–10, 14, 17, 65–6, 68–70, 73–4, 108, 118, 145, 148
omnipotent(ence) 38, 53
oral 52
organic 10, 65
outline 68, 87
overflow 42, 55, 67, 69–70
overwhelm 7, 20, 35, 68, 78–9, 81–3, 94, 107, 116, 133, 141

panic 24, 27, 58, 66, 72–3
paralysis 15, 20, 24, 26, 116, 137
paranoid 126, 130; paranoid-schizoid 65
parental dyad/couple 15, 96, 98–9, 101
Patterson, Z. 17, 134, 148
Pecotic, B. 37, 50
PECS 141
Perry, C. 6–7, 17
persecutory 76, 79, 83
personal signature 108
phallus 122
phatic communication 143
phenomenological i, 134
phonophobia 25
photo 29, 31, 33, 141; photo album 28
play 2, 3, 8, 10, 14, 32, 46, 49, 60, 69, 76–8, 81, 84–5, 90, 97, 100, 103, 110, 115–18, 123, 131, 138–9, 141, 143, 14, 149; playful 31, 49, 76–7, 84, 113, 115, 141
plug 67
potential space 8, 11, 29, 39, 46, 49, 99, 116, 129, 131, 143
power 28, 30, 53, 58, 63, 139; disempower 99; empower 63
pre-attentive images 133
preconscious 67, 72
pre-representational 21, 90, 116
pre-symbolic 65, 73, 116

primary; primary consciousness 146; primary identification 86; primary process 82, 145; primary self 81
primitive 17, 22, 46, 49, 63, 65, 74, 118, 148; primitive communications 49, 137–8
process xi, 5–8, 10, 12–14, 18–19, 22, 26, 28, 30, 32, 35–8, 42, 46–7, 49, 58, 65–9, 74–6, 80–2, 85–7, 89, 91, 94, 100–2, 105, 107–8, 111, 113, 115–18, 120–1, 123–4, 129–30, 133–4, 136–140, 142, 147, 149
professional identity 8, 75–6, 79
project 24, 42, 83–4, 115, 117; projection 137–8
projective identification 138, 148
psyche 82, 86–7; psyche/soma 79, 82, 86
psychic coherence 9, 13, 145
psychic space 31, 79
psychoanalytic xi, 5–6, 9–10, 12, 17, 49, 65, 86, 118, 134, 136, 142, 145, 147–9
psychodynamic xi, 5, 7, 9, 15, 20–1, 30, 32, 49, 53, 60, 63, 67, 86, 102, 116, 137, 142, 146
psychogenic 9–10, 136
psychologist 3, 12, 31, 100, 143
psychotic 18, 121, 125, 130

Rabiger, S. 99, 103
rage 39, 79, 110
Randomised Controlled Trials 146
Real, the 75, 138
reality principle 53
reality testing 133, 140
reciprocal relationship 83
re-constellation 82
Rees, M. 16–17, 33, 50, 63, 102–3, 131
reflective function 87

regression 117, 140
Reid, S. 5, 16, 42, 49–50
relationship based therapy 130
reparation 85, 115
repeated 45, 52, 55–6, 58–9, 61, 77, 127
research i, xi, 2, 73, 85, 87, 100, 102, 116–7
resistance 13, 19–20, 31, 33, 68, 99
restraint 89
reverie 9, 36, 68, 70, 81, 138, 145
rhythm 10, 13–14, 20, 25, 38, 49, 66, 71–3
rigid 9–10, 14, 20, 37, 76–8, 82–4, 92, 97, 109, 122, 143
ritual 4–5, 15, 21, 41, 67, 69, 76, 141
Rorschach inkblots 24
Rostron, J. 17, 73–4, 94, 103, 131, 134–5, 146, 148
routine 11, 14, 37–8, 41, 47, 51, 53, 55–6, 58–9, 76, 117
RS-Index 105, 118
running 41–2, 45, 72, 127–8; running water 62, 70
Rutten-Saris, M. 12, 16, 23, 25, 28, 33, 39, 50, 105, 118
Rutter, M. 2, 17
Rycroft, C. 53, 63

Schaverien, J. 11, 17, 78, 88
schema xiii, 15, 43, 105, 117, 140; schematic 45
schizophrenia 2, 16, 76–7
Schore, A. 144, 146
scribble 43, 55, 57, 59–61, 107–8
Sacks, O. 4, 17, 138, 146, 148
Samuels, A. 86, 88
second skin 10, 41
Segal, H. 11, 17, 131
self 2–3, 10, 12–13, 15–16, 29, 36, 45, 50, 57, 59, 76, 78–9, 81–2, 85–7, 113, 115, 117, 119, 122, 124, 129, 136, 139, 144, 146; false self 50, 78; *self and other* 10, 12, 76, 144;

self-esteem 127; self-experience 115; self-portrait 110; sense of self 12, 36, 50, 57, 79, 86, 113, 117, 129, 139
sense impression 66, 72, 138
sensory 4, 7, 9, 12, 25, 39, 41–2, 65, 68; *sensory impression* 65
sensual 59, 69, 139
separateness 9, 26, 29, 48, 120
severe learning difficulties 89–90, 101–3, 117, 140, 143
sexuality 90, 120, 122–3
shame 84
shape 24, 53, 66, 68–9, 72, 83–4, 91–2, 95, 97–8
shared space 46, 80
sharing 10, 12, 15–16, 21, 27, 33, 36–7, 53, 84, 94, 96, 129, 134, 147
Siegel, D. 144, 146
silence 13, 23, 25, 35–7, 48–9, 122, 140
Simon, R. v, 105, 137, 148
Sinason, V. 120, 122, 131
sister 106, 121
Skaife, S. 17, 134, 148
skin 10, 41, 49, 66, 69–70, 72, 122, 124–5
social interaction 3–4, 12, 49, 118, 142–3
Solms, M. 117–18, 145–6, 148
space 5, 8, 13, 16, 21–3, 31, 33, 35–7, 39–43, 45–50, 62–3, 66, 70, 78–82, 90, 92, 96, 98–9, 102, 108, 111, 115–16, 120–1, 129–31, 139, 142, 144
specular image 86, 139
speech & language therapist 89, 102
spilling 39–40, 42–3, 83
split 23, 79, 134
spoken language 25
spontaneity 2, 14, 62, 84–5, 97, 141
Springham, N. 144, 148
Squiggle game 137

Stack, M. 12, 17, 22, 24, 33, 94, 99, 103, 131
Star Wars 133
stencils 91–2, 95–8
Stern, D. 12–13, 17, 22, 32, 36, 39, 50, 73–4, 105, 108, 113, 117–18, 133–4, 136–7, 145–6, 148
Still, C. 107
Stott, J. & Males, B. 131
stress 19–20, 37, 76
subjectivity 81, 87, 136, 138
supervisor/supervision 23, 26–8, 31–2, 51, 53, 56–7, 60, 97, 101–2, 105, 111, 120, 122, 127, 129, 142
symbiotic relationship 25
symbol formation 1, 8, 10–11, 17, 131
symbolic 1, 8, 10–15, 19, 24, 28–9, 30, 43, 49–50, 75–6, 79, 84, 108, 113, 115, 123, 129, 138–40, 142–3, 146, 148
symbolic equation xiv, 11
Symbolic, the 14, 138–9, 142

tactile 52
Tantam, D. 20, 33
Takeda, F. 137, 148
Tavistock Autism Workshop 5, 16
teeth 93, 125
theoretical i, xi, 1, 14, 16, 63, 65, 76, 81, 85, 105, 115, 133
Theory of Mind 4, 16, 20, 144–5, 147
therapeutic relationship 8, 15, 29, 46, 89–90, 119–20, 129, 135, 139–40
think, capacity to 79; *think together* 37, 100, 105
third area 8, 75, 85, 142–3; third person 90, 93
time 5, 7, 14, 24, 55, 66, 69, 72, 115; sense of time 24, 69; time out 39, 45

Tipple, R. 11, 18, 32–3, 99, 103, 131, 133–4, 149
toilet 41–2, 55, 61, 67, 107
training 7, 19, 51, 62–3, 90, 101, 129
transcendent function 8, 17, 75, 87
transference 5–6, 9, 17, 32, 101, 134, 136–7, 142
transformation 8, 52, 76
transitional 29, 115, 131
translation 134
trauma 9, 14, 24, 50, 65, 76, 120
triad 1, 3, 5, 18–19, 141–2
triangulation 105, 141–2
trust 41, 57, 61, 76, 105, 113, 119, 121, 134
Tustin, F. 9, 18, 24, 37, 42, 50, 66, 72–4, 105–6, 108, 110, 118, 120, 124, 131, 145, 149
twin 121, 124
tyranny 70

unconnected 80, 86
unconscious xi, 5–7, 10, 26, 37, 53, 66, 72, 86–7, 94, 118, 122–3, 126, 137–8, 142, 145–6
Urwin, C. 142–3, 145, 149

verbal 8, 19–20, 24, 31, 81, 84, 89, 96–7, 99, 107, 123, 129, 134, 140; non-verbal 3, 42, 54, 136, 143; pre-verbal 12, 36, 37, 43, 89, 135; verbal interaction 97; verbalisation 107; *verbal self* 115
video 74, 133–4, 142
violent 41, 85, 89, 100, 110
visual thinking 31, 141
vitality affects 16, 33, 39, 50, 105
vocalisation 25, 90, 113, 143
voices 77, 79, 81, 83–4
void 36, 39, 41–2, 118
Volkmar, F. 3, 18, 21, 24, 33
vulnerable 95, 145
Vygotsky, L. 143, 149

wavelength 48–9
Weiser, J. 29, 33
well-being 62, 74, 130
Williams, D. 18, 124, 131, 135
Wing, L. 1, 3, 18, 33, 121, 131, 141
Winnicott, D.W. 8, 10, 14, 18, 46, 50, 65–6, 73–4, 99–100, 103, 105, 115–16, 118, 129, 131, 137, 143, 149
'wiped out' 90, 94, 137–8
Wright, K. 57, 63, 105, 118

ZPD 143